P9-DUT-099

The Gospel
and the Sacred

From the
Library of:

Brother Mark McVann
F.S.C.

The Gospel
and the Sacred
Poetics of Violence in Mark

ROBERT G. HAMERTON-KELLY

Fortress Press   Minneapolis

For my mother

THE GOSPEL AND THE SACRED
Poetics of Violence in Mark

Copyright © 1994 Augsburg Fortress. All rights reserved. Except for brief quotations in critical articles or reviews, no part of this book may be reproduced in any manner without prior written permission from the publisher. Write to: Permissions, Augsburg Fortress, 426 S. Fifth St., Box 1209, Minneapolis, MN 55440.

Scripture quotations, unless otherwise noted, are the author's translation.

Cover design: Nancy Eato, Neato Design
Cover art: El Greco, "Christ Driving the Money Changers from the Temple," used by permission of The Minneapolis Institute of Arts.

Library of Congress Cataloging-in-Publication Data

Hamerton-Kelly, Robert
    The gospel and the sacred : poetics of violence in Mark / Robert
G. Hamerton-Kelly.
        p.   cm.
    Includes bibliographical references and index.
    ISBN 0-8006-2669-9 :
    1. Bible. N. T. Mark—Criticism, Narrative. 2. Violence—
Religious aspects. 3. Scapegoat. 4. Gerard, René, 1923–
I. Title.
BS2585.6.V55H35   1994   93-22398
226.3'066—dc20   CIP

The paper used in this publication meets the minimum requirements of American National Standard for Information Sciences—Permanence of Paper for Printed Library Materials, ANSI Z329.48-1984. ∞™

Manufactured in the U.S.A.   AF 1-2669

98   97   96   95   94   1   2   3   4   5   6   7   8   9   10

Contents

Foreword

The problem with interdisciplinary theories is the distrust that they in-spire in serious scholars in the various fields which the theorists uncere-moniously invade. The insiders understandably resent the invasion, and the temptation to dismiss the invaders out of hand is almost irresistible.

For many years, I have been myself in the situation of the unwanted outsider. I am not a New Testament scholar but at a crucial point in the elaboration of the mimetic theory, I realized that the four Gospels play a crucial role in it and I focused on them more and more. On the whole, the scholars in that field have been more open to the new mimetic idea than the specialists of some other fields. They are quite aware, however, that the mimetic theory lacks the scholarly backing it should have before it can be regarded as a serious hypothesis in their field.

For the future of the theory, it is essential that its claims be critically assessed by New Testament scholars of the highest caliber. This is what the present book is about, at least in part. It is the work of a highly com-petent New Testament specialist who interprets in the light of the mimetic theory not some selected passages of Mark, as I have done, but the entire Gospel. Robert Hamerton-Kelly brings to this task his superb linguistic expertise, his vast historical and theological background, and his great familiarity with the scholarly literature in the field.

In the past ten years, Robert Hamerton-Kelly has become personally committed to the mimetic theory and has published a book on Paul which is influenced by it (*Sacred Violence: Paul's Hermeneutic of the Cross*

[Minneapolis: Fortress Press, 1992]). This fact does not make what I just said any less true, of course. When this author first embraced the mimetic theory, he already was a remarkably trained New Testament scholar. His study of Mark reinforces the conclusion to which his study of Paul had already led him. There is nothing in the mimetic theory that contradicts the requirements of sound scholarship and there is a great deal that can help us reach a better understanding of Christian Scripture.

Robert Hamerton-Kelly is not a New Testament scholar only. He is also a social scientist and a literary critic, and these additional talents make him even more, rather than less, competent as a scholar. They also affect his relationship to the mimetic theory, which is more original and creative than his modesty allows him to say. It would be grossly unfair, therefore, to present this book as a mere scholarly *imprimatur* given to the mimetic theory. The author's new insights are too numerous for quick summarization and some are only indirectly related to the mimetic theory. These include a development of the poetics of time and space, a discussion of architectural metaphors, and a most remarkable view of the total Gospel's composition as an endlessly ascending spiral. This view plays a role in the unusual composition of the book.

Instead of merely following the Gospel from beginning to end, the book begins with the so-called cleansing of the temple, which is interpreted as an attack against the Jewish sacrificial system as a whole. The analysis is pursued until the end of the Gospel and then it circles back to the beginning, and the first eleven chapters are read in the light of the insights gained from the account of the crucifixion.

The main theological insight is the nonsacrificial view of redemption. Sacrificial violence is not absent from the Gospel but it is reserved to human beings. Jesus gives his life to men and not to a vengeful God. It is nevertheless legitimate to say that he gives his life to God "in the secondary sense that [Jesus'] service for us is done for the sake of God." The language of substitution remains perfectly acceptable. Far from contradicting the traditional formulations of the Christian faith, the mimetic interpretation vindicates them. This vindication is one of the most interesting and paradoxical consequences of the mimetic reading, which is radical and subversive in a more authentic sense than the conventional subversiveness of our time. As a result, the book often has a slightly ironic flavor that will give it piquancy and charm in the eyes of the more discriminating readers.

This vindication of many traditional attitudes is one of the reasons, perhaps, why the mimetic theory rubs so many people the wrong way.

Another reason is that many people have only a secondhand and highly misleading acquaintance with that theory. They tend to reduce it to some kind of narrative or to some other theory that is also primarily a narrative, such as the anthropology of *Totem and Taboo.*

The mimetic theory is not abstruse, but one cannot dispense with a firsthand knowledge of it. One must be able to retrace the very simple but logically interconnected steps that lead from mimetic rivalry to the mimetic or sacrificial crisis and then, from that crisis, to what Hamerton-Kelly calls the GMSM: generative mimetic scapegoating mechanism.

The number one reason why the theory is misunderstood is a widespread failure to realize what the word *generative* entails. Critics expect scapegoats to show up as such in the texts they generate—dressed up in some kind of scapegoat uniform, I suppose. When they find no such thing, they loudly proclaim the bankruptcy of the theory. There can be only indirect clues to the GMSM, such as the guilt of Oedipus, or his alleged responsibility for the Theban plague, or his clubfoot, and so on. The only texts that make scapegoating completely explicit are the Gospels, and that is why they are truly unique. They, alone, are not structured by the GMSM.

Mimetic theory is too realistic and commensensical to be confused with one more nihilistic stepchild of German idealism. And yet, unlike the positivistic social sciences, it is not blind to paradox; it can articulate the intricacies of human relations just as effectively as a Kierkegaard or a Dostoievsky.

Unlike the whole Nietzschean–Heideggerian deconstructive tradition, mimetic theory is not contemptuous of science; yet, unlike the social sciences, it is not tempted to ape the methods of the natural sciences. It has more interesting things to do and it does them on its own, with its own independent resources.

Of most theories, such as psychoanalysis or structuralism, it is legitimate to say that they are "applied" to the Gospels. In the case of mimetic theory, the language of "application" falters. Whenever the theory is used as intelligently as it is in this book, it tends to disappear behind the text. It is so close to the text that, when the two are brought together, the text wins out. The theory dissolves into the text, and this annihilation is its greatest triumph.

A good example of this is *skandalon,* a word systematically ignored by centuries of exegesis and commentaries, in spite of its unquestionable importance. Its frequency in all four Gospels and the diversity of its uses designate it as a major enigma that is never scrutinized for the simple reason that, until now, no solution seemed possible.

Skandalon designates the obstacle that mimetic models become when their desires clash with their imitators' desires and, instead of being discouraged by the clash, the imitation intensifies, generating a vicious circle of frustrated fascination that can only lead to violence and destruction.

Do we have a name for the kind of interpretation that this book exemplifies? Hamerton-Kelly calls it a hermeneutics of sacred violence and I have no better label to offer. But this is hermeneutics with a backbone—a far cry from the old kind, which has been somewhat discredited by its excessive limpness and pliability.

The sign that new knowledge is being produced is easily mistaken for a sign of no knowledge at all. It cannot fit any of the compartments in which the old knowledge was distributed. The knowledge in this book is not new in the sense that it would change or add anything to the Gospel of Mark, but it is new in the sense of opening up areas of the Gospels that had been closed until now, at least to rational discourse.

The parable of the new wine and the old wineskins is the perfect metaphor for the problem we all have with genuine novelty. As this problem gets worse, we need the parable more and more but we are less and less able to hear it. The new wine is "always already" spilled and we do not realize that we, ourselves, spilled it. We maintain that the old vineyard cannot produce any new wine. . . . The readers of this book will make no such mistake. They will have their new containers ready for the new wine and they will find it even better than the old.

RENÉ GIRARD

Abbreviations

BETL	Bibliotheca ephemeridum theologicarum lovaniensium
GMSM	René Girard's concept of the "generative mimetic scapegoating mechanism"; see Appendix
HNT	Handbuch sum Neuen Testament
HTR	*Harvard Theological Review*
JBL	*Journal of Biblical Literature*
JNES	*Journal of Near Eastern Studies*
JSS	*Journal of Semitic Studies*
LXX	The Septuagint
MT	The Masoretic Text
NTS	*New Testament Studies*
SBLDS	Society of Biblical Literature Dissertation Series

Preface

In *Sacred Violence: Paul's Hermeneutic of the Cross* (Minneapolis: Fortress, 1992), I attempted a reading of the Pauline text through the lens of René Girard's theory of violence and the sacred. This book is an attempt to do the same for the text of Mark. The two books might, therefore, be read together as examples of the Girardian method at work in the interpretation of New Testament discourse and narrative texts, respectively. The present book is mostly a commentary on the text and should, therefore, be read with the (Greek) text of the Gospel at hand.

The appendix gives a brief summary of the theory and its application, and might serve to introduce students and others to its basic elements. The reading that it makes possible here must stand as the recommendation for such an effort. Full bibliographic citations for the notes are provided in the Bibliography.

Many people have helped me in thinking about the issues of interpretation at stake here. I have learned most from René Girard, my colleague at Stanford. His friendship has been an inspiration, and his biweekly seminar for visiting scholars and others, held at the Center for International Security and Arms Control, has been a constant source of information and insight from many different fields of study. Recently, I have profited from conversations with H. J. Lundager Jensen of Aarhus University and James Williams of Syracuse University during their time as visiting scholars in the Program of Interdisciplinary Research at Stanford and later in Aarhus and at meetings of the Colloquium on Violence and Religion. I thank

them for their help. The Colloquium on Violence and Religion, organized around the thought of René Girard, has been a source of inspiration
and insight, and I thank my colleagues from many disciplines, who make
up its membership, for their support, especially the president, Raymund
Schwager, and the editor of the bulletin, Wolfgang Palaver. I thank Walter
Wink of Auburn Theological Seminary for helpful comments based on
the reading of an earlier draft. I have rewritten the text several times since
then and his comments have found their place in the rewritings. Finally, I
thank two ladies without whom the book would not have been written at
all: Grace Mortsolf, who has supported my work at the Center for several
years, and my mother, Joan Hobbs, to whom I dedicate the work.

Earlier versions of some of the material were published as: "Die
>Menschenmenge< und die Poetik des Sündenbocks im Markusevan-
gelium," in *Dramatische Erlöungslehre: Ein Symposion,* ed. J. Niewiadomski
and W. Palaver (Innsbruck-Wien: Tyrolia, 1992) 49–70, and "Sacred Violence and the Messiah: The Markan Passion Narrative as a Redefinition
of Messianology," in *The Messiah: Developments in Earliest Judaism and
Christianity,* ed. J. H. Charlesworth (Minneapolis: Fortress, 1992) 461–
93. The material has been rewritten and in some places changed signifi-
cantly in being integrated into the present text.

My colleagues at the Center for International Security and Arms
Control have been most patient with my pursuit of gospel knowledge
amid the discussions of defense restructuring, regional conflicts, and
military intervention. They know that there is a baleful link between
violence and religion and therefore thought it worthwhile that one of
their members should think theoretically about the problem. I thank
them all for their support, especially David Holloway and Michael May,
co-directors, and Coit Blacker, director of studies.

Introduction

The Theory of Sacred Violence as a Method of Interpretation

The temple is the central symbol in the Gospel[1] of Mark because it is the focal point of the passion.[2] All the action leading up to the death of Jesus (chaps. 11–15) takes place either in relation to the temple or in the temple precinct itself. The account of the passion begins with the "cleansing" of the temple (chap. 11), pivots on the prophecy of its destruction (chap. 13), and summarizes the false accusations against Jesus at his "trial" before the Sanhedrin in the claim that he threatened to destroy the temple (14:58). Jesus died as a result of a conflict with the temple.

The driving out of the money changers and victim mongers, usually referred to as the "cleansing" of the temple (11:15-19), seals his fate. It is an act of prophetic symbolism that declares the end of the sacrificial system,[3] and it is the most fruitful point of departure for an understanding of Mark's Gospel.

---

[1] I use Gospel with a G to indicate the Gospel of Mark, or the other written Gospels, and gospel with a lower case *g* to indicate the power that generates the Gospel text and is the counterpart to the generative mimetic scapegoating mechanism (GMSM).

[2] D. Juel, *Messiah and Temple*. See also J. H. Elliott, "Social Scientific Criticism," 21, who criticizes Gerd Theissen for neglecting the tension between the temple and various groups, "Patterns in the evidence brought to light by the matrix, furthermore, reveal how the temple was a focal point of tension (political, economic, social, cultural and ideological)."

[3] E. P. Sanders, *Jesus and Judaism*, 75: "Thus we conclude that Jesus publicly predicted or threatened the destruction of the temple, that the statement was shaped by his expectation of the arrival of the eschaton, that he probably also expected a new temple to be given by God from heaven, and that he made a demonstration which prophetically symbolized the coming

The Gospel of Mark was probably written in the aftermath of the Roman destruction of the temple in 70 C.E.[4] It sees that destruction as a judgment on the kind of religion represented by the temple. Traditional anthropology designates this kind of religion as the manifestation and service of the "Sacred." This is the sense in which I use the term *Sacred,* and I see it as the source of the ordering powers of society. The place of the Sacred is the place of sacrifice and it provides the center of a topology of significance because it is the pivot of sacred space around which the community is topographically and psychologically organized. The "cleansing" of the temple is a symbol of the rejection of the Sacred and the denial of its place at the center of significance. *Significance from now on is eccentric; there is to be no holy city, no holy land, and, by implication, no chosen people.* In Christ all are chosen for salvation and so no one is especially chosen.

The rending of the sanctuary's veil at the moment of Jesus' death confirms this symbolic message. It shows that the sanctuary is empty—"there is no there there"—and prompts the centurion's confession that God is present on the cross and accessible to the Gentiles, even to a Roman executioner (15:38-39). The tension between Jesus and the temple, therefore, is the central relationship in the narrative. It is the tension between the gospel and the Sacred and in order to understand the Gospel of Mark we need a theory of the Sacred that will help us to interpret its poetics.

The term *poetics* comes from structuralism and describes the insight that texts are made (ποίειν) by powers that work unseen beneath the surface. Scientifically, it refers to capacities like transcendental linguistic competencies or constant characteristics of human psychological or social behavior that structure communication. These unseen powers, however, have a sinister reputation in some quarters. They deliberately deform communication in the service of self-interest. For psychoanalysis, they deform the expression of sexuality because of shame; for Marxism, they deform the expression of political interest because of greed. I share this suspicion of the powers of poiesis. I believe they are, for the most part, in the propaganda ministry of violence, and that the gospel discloses and counters this propaganda.

The poetics of violence that generates the idea of sacred space is a timely topic. The religio-nationalist ideology that is currently causing

---

event." It is not necessary for my purpose to decide whether it was an act of the historical Jesus nor to ascertain whether the historical Jesus rejected the temple and the system of sacrifice. All I maintain is that the text before us rejects the temple and its sacrifices.

[4]J. Marcus, "The Jewish War."

bloodshed in the Middle East, the Balkans, and elsewhere is a product of this poiesis, and the Bible is an important source of its thematic expression. I believe that we can understand the generative mechanism of this poiesis because it is disclosed by great literary and religious texts. The biblical texts that tell of a promised land and a chosen people are offset by the Gospel text that rejects both notions by showing that they are essentially disguises for scapegoating violence. There is, therefore, a political issue at stake in the reading I propose. If the gospel is what I say it is, then Christianity must sustain a searching criticism of all ethnic and nationalist claims, whether made in the name of Christianity, or Judaism, or Islam, or self-determination, or ethnic pride, or patriotism, or whatever other ideology is made to serve as a veil for violence, in the name of the universal eccentricity of the gospel.

I believe that the Sacred is violence operating as religion by the ruse of scapegoating substitution. The money changers and victim mongers in the temple symbolize a conception of the Sacred that links substitution and violence. They represent the sacrificial system[5] because it is a system of substitution, and money and victims are substitutes. In the movement through the religious system from the offerer to the victim, there are three moments of substitution. The process begins with the profane currency that the worshiper brings to the temple to purchase a sacrificial victim. The first moment is the substitution of this money for the self. It takes the place of labor, goods, or real property, and represents the self. The second moment is the substitution of the sacred money of the temple for this profane money, and the third moment is the substitution of the victim for the sacred money. By this threefold substitution, the sacrificial system separates the self of the offerer by two stages from the body of the victim, and three stages from the god who receives the offering. The victim represents the offerer to the god at third remove through a scrim of substitution that enables the offerer to dissociate from the violence of the sacrifice while ensuring that the violence takes place and its benefits accrue.[6]

In the narrative of the "cleansing," money is therefore a symbol of the refusal to take responsibility for violence. By linking money with sacrifice and making the "cleansing" of the temple symbolic of the rejection of the sacrificial system, the narrative interprets sacrificial substitution as a

---

[5] Sanders, *Jesus and Judaism,* 69–71; M. Borg, *Conflict, Holiness and Politics,* 171–73.

[6] B. Chilton, *The Temple of Jesus,* 128, believes that Jesus was motivated chiefly by the fact that the substitution of money removed the offerer too far from the offering, turning sacrifice into "a purely financial transaction."

denial of responsibility and suggests that René Girard's[7] theory of the Sacred as violence denied and disguised might be fruitful for an understanding of the gospel.

We present, therefore, by way of introduction, a brief account of Girard's theory, because we intend to take it as a guide to our interpretation.[8]

Mimetic Desire

In the West, desire has been recognized as a central element in human conduct and self-understanding ever since Paul located the human problem in the field of desire (Rom 7:7).[9] Augustine took desire as a guide to the relationship between the soul and God, Hegel made it central to the philosophy of consciousness, and Freud used it in the interpretation of dreams and "hysterical" symptoms. Girard traces the ways of desire by means of ethology, anthropology, and, above all, great literature.

The two most evident manifestations of desire in human relations are *vengeance* and *scapegoating*. When these fail they become *resentment,* as the energy of vengeance and scapegoating turns back upon the subject and causes self-wounding and self-scapegoating. These three ugly siblings are present in all human relations. They are the essence of banality and the key to the individual and society and the interaction between the two. They are produced by the system of desire functioning through a generative mechanism.

Girard hypothesizes that desire finds its object by imitating the desire of others and that this imitativeness is rooted in phylogeny. The higher primates have strong imitative impulses and these become stronger as the threshold of hominization is crossed. At the human level, imitation becomes desire; Girard calls this imitative desire mimesis. Mimesis operates initially below the level of consciousness, but is not a biological drive like Freud's libido. Mimesis is rather an interpersonal attraction rooted more in psychosocial reality than in biology, although it has a power comparable to a biological drive. It is a

---

[7] See the appendix; see also: R. Girard, *Deceit, Desire, and the Novel; Violence and the Sacred; To Double Business Bound; The Scapegoat; Things Hidden Since the Foundation of the World;* (with J.-M. Oughourlian, and G. Lefort); *A Theater of Envy;* (ed. R. G. Hamerton-Kelly) *Violent Origins;* (ed. P. Dumouchel) *Violence and Truth.*

[8] For a longer account, see the Appendix.

[9] See R. G. Hamerton-Kelly, *Sacred Violence.*

way persons affect and relate to each other, and is in principle suscepti-
ble to moral intervention.

At the human level, mimesis is, first, *acquisitive,* because desire copies
the desire of another for an object. Acquisitive desire is, therefore, *mediated through a model* whose desire is copied. One can represent this desire
as triangular: the model that desire imitates is at the apex of the triangle,
and desire and the object are at the respective angles of the base.

The size of the base angles, then, controls the distance between the
model and desire. The larger the angles and farther away the model,
the smoother the mediation. So, for instance, a model far exalted in
status above the imitator does not often become a rival for an object.
Girard calls this *external mediation.*

Internal mediation, on the other hand, occurs when the angles narrow
and draw the model so near to the baseline that it becomes an *obstacle,* in
the sense of a rival, to the fulfillment of desire. Because the model and
the imitator are virtually equal in status, they are rivals for the object. In
this case, the model ultimately comes between the imitator and the object, and changes from a model to an obstacle. Desire then shifts its aim
from the object to the model/obstacle and acquisitive desire becomes
sheer *rivalry,* which contests recognition and status rather than possession
of the object.

The Crisis of Differentiation and the Generative
Mimetic Scapegoating Mechanism (GMSM)

At this point, mimesis has passed from the acquisitive to the *conflictual*
mode producing the violence that destroys cultural distinctions. The
erasure of distinctions makes culture impossible, and disordered perception causes monsters to appear because the differences between humans
and animals are no longer clear. This is the *crisis of differentiation* that
Girard calls the "sacrificial crisis," or the "mimetic crisis."

Because differentiation is culture's supporting skeleton, there had to
be, in the course of development, a way of restoring the distinctions that
violence erased, and it had to be a cultural device because prehominid
dominance patterns and automatic hierarchies do not work for humans.[10]

---

[10] The increased power of imitation in humans can probably be correlated with the
growth of the human brain and the consequent enhancement of the imitative energy. In
prehominid bands, mimetic rivalry does not reach the point of crisis because the simian

The cultural device in this case was the *generative mimetic scapegoating mechanism (GMSM)* that arises from within the crisis of differentiation as a spontaneous metamorphosis of the system.[11]

The GMSM works as follows: While, on the one hand, mimetic enthrallment with the model/obstacle diverts attention from the object, the GMSM, on the other, rediscovers the object, but now as something to be destroyed rather than possessed. The rivals displace their violence toward one another onto a surrogate victim who has been *substituted* for the original object of mimetic desire. The killing of the victim thus spontaneously unites the rivals. The violence that divided them as rivals now unites them as accomplices. It remains the same energy of mimetic desire but its goal has changed twice: from the original object that it fixed on by imitating the model to the model-become-rival, and then to the victim substituted for the original object, which makes the model no longer a rival but an accomplice. The first unity is, therefore, the unity of the lynch mob.

This spontaneous unity is the necessary condition for the reinstitution of differentiation, and differentiation is necessary for culture. Culture, therefore, comes from the victim. Mimetic rivalry erases differences and makes the combatants "doubles" of one another. They become rivals as they succeed in imitating one another, and successful imitation means doubling. Thus, violence erases difference.

The GMSM, which comes into being as a result of this spontaneous change in the system of desire first puts an end to the bad violence of mimetic rivalry by the "good" violence of surrogate victimage, and establishes the unity of the lynch mob. Then it uses the difference between the two kinds of violence and the difference between the mob and the victim as the fundamental differences on which to build all subsequent cultural differentiation. Culture comes from the "lamb slain since the foundation of the world" (Rev 13:8), because differentiation ramifies from the victim.

The GMSM is, therefore, the mechanism of surrogate victimage that controls the violence of mimetic desire and transforms it from disordering into ordering power. It is *generative* because it generates the differences, it is mimetic because *mimetic* desire (not sexuality) drives it, it is *scapegoating*

---

brain does not generate the same amplitude of imitative energy as the larger human brain. Therefore, in animal groups, patterns of dominance can be established within the existing system, while human groups need some new ordering factor.

[11] At this point, the link to systems theory becomes evident; see H. Atlan and J.-P. Dupuy, "Mimesis and Social Morphogenesis," and J.-P. Dupuy, *Ordres et Desordres*. Dupuy's ideas of "tangled hierarchy" (e.g., Escher's "Hands") and "endogenous fixed points" are particularly pertinent here.

because it achieves its purpose by striking the surrogate victim; and it is *a mechanism* because it operates like a machine, systemically rather than deliberately. It is important to emphasize that the energy is mimetic and not sexual because that difference sets it off from psychoanalysis, with which it is sometimes confused. The Oedipus myth, which is the defining model for psychoanalysis, is primarily a myth of mimetic desire and scapegoating, not of parricide and incest. Parricide and incest are functions of mimesis and scapegoating, not originary mechanisms.

The Double Transference and the Primitive Sacred

The category of the Sacred designates the process by which differentiation is instituted on the basis of the difference between the victim and the mob. In the moment of peace that follows the killing, the mob mistakenly attributes the cause of peace to the victim rather than to themselves. They transfer their mimetic rivalry and their need of the surrogate to the victim. The victim, not they themselves, caused mimetic violence and demanded the killing of victims to stop it. This must be true because there was disorder while the victim lived and order when the victim died. This *double transference*—of the mob's mimetic rivalry and its need for a surrogate to bring peace—therefore makes the victim, who is at most a catalyst, into an active cause, conceals violence from its source, and creates a fiction to represent it. It transforms the victim into the god, the mighty one who causes disorder and brings order.

The result of the double transference is the primitive *Sacred* with its well-known powers of threat and succor, which is *the victim transformed by the double transference into the god*. The Sacred, in turn, provides the energy and structure of social order through its primary manifestations of prohibition, ritual, and myth, the first two of which are the transferred elements of the mob's own violence, of its disordering and ordering powers. *Prohibition* issues from the mimetic rivalry pole of the Sacred to forbid any behavior that might cause that rivalry to break out again. *Ritual* issues from the surrogate victim pole as the controlled repetition of the founding murder in the form of ritual sacrifice, with a view to renewing the ordering energy of surrogate victimage. *Myth* emerges as the account of the founding murder told from the point of view of the murderers, as part of the transformation of the victim into the god.

The victim is the first transcendental signifier, and so representation (substitution) is also the result of violence. The first representation is the misrepresentation of the victim as violent and dangerous. The sudden peace that followed the death made the victim the first object of a briefly nonmimetic attention, the first "other" to which we can point and from which we can receive signification. What is signified is the mimetic violence and surrogate victimage that goes out to the victim as violence and comes back as prohibition, ritual, and myth; out as disorder and back as order. Thus, differential thought and representation originate in the logic of the exception—of the one who is different and expelled—rather than the logic of structuralism's binary opposites.

The Sacred, therefore, is the fiction of founding violence created by this double transference of mimetic rivalry and surrogate victimage from the mob to the victim. By blaming the victim, the mob covers up its own violence against one another (vengeance) and its scapegoating of the victim. The task of a critical interpretation of culture is to decipher this fiction which has been encoded with guile and must be decoded with double guile.[12] The system of the Sacred, therefore, is based on the self-deception that the energy of the system is not our violence but the violence of the god. It pretends that the god demands victims, to maintain the order of good violence. Thus, the order of existing culture is an order of sacred violence centered on the place of sacrifice and sustained by the threat (prohibition), the promise (ritual), and the lie (myth). The threat is the menace of the god's vengeance should the prohibition be transgressed and the transgression remain unappeased. The promise is the propitiatory and prophylactic power of ritual sacrifice that renews the threatened order. The lie is the myth that represents this order as benign and justifies the killing of victims. The task of a cultural criticism is to demythologize the threat, the promise, and the lie, in institutions, offices, and texts, by exposing the victim on which they are founded.

The GMSM and the Category of Sacrifice

It is a mistake to see the GMSM as tied to the category of sacrifice.[13] Like several other traditional categories, the category of sacrifice is vague in present anthropology,[14] because the phenomena it used to encompass are now seen to overflow the boundaries of several categories. To make the

---

[12] The phrase belongs to P. Ricoeur, *Freud and Philosophy.*

[13] Chilton, *The Temple of Jesus,* makes this mistake and understands Girard to be proposing a theory of sacrifice alongside other theories.

[14] M. Bloch, *Prey into Hunter,* 25.

GMSM a theory of sacrifice would, therefore, tie it to the problematic past of anthropology. The GMSM is a generative mechanism of the psychosocial system of desire whose action can be traced in all kinds of ethnographic and literary texts. Ritual is one mode of its manifestation, and rituals called sacrifice show its generative influence in different ways. The close correlation between the GMSM and the category of sacrifice in the Gospel of Mark is due to the centrality of the temple in that narrative.

The Nature and Sources of the Theory

Scapegoating is a more appropriate description of the mechanism than sacrifice, because in current usage scapegoating covers a wide variety of actions and attitudes that occur in literature, politics, and academic committees. Girard does not, therefore, make the Judeo-Christian understanding of sacrifice the standard by which to judge whether an African ritual is to be called "sacrifice" or not,[15] but rather regards the Judeo-Christian sacrifice as a prime trace of the GMSM.

Girard is reluctant to call his hypothesis a theory, because he does not want it to be classified along with the many ephemeral modes of interpretation that are included under the rubric of "literary theory." The knowledge on which the hypothesis is based is banal and self-evident, like the knowledge that the accusations of witchcraft were bogus and that the Jews did not cause the Black Death, nor cannibalize Christian children, nor poison the wells. The theory rests on the knowledge we now have of the scapegoating impulse and the function of a certain kind of discourse, which Girard calls mythic, to occlude and justify this violence. It is evident in the anthropological and psychological understanding we now have of sorcery as the accusation that a randomly chosen individual has the power and the ill-will to cause the disaster in question.[16] The theory is, in fact, evident in every human interaction or institution as envy, revenge, eroticism, sado-masochism, resentment, ambition, and the other energies of disordered desire in search of a victim.

In simplest terms, the theory of the GMSM is an explanation of what it is that generates human relations as that may be gleaned from common experience and a few great works of literature—not all literature but

---

[15] Marcel Detienne believes that Girard simply brings the crypto-Christianity of the tradition that derives from Marcel Mauss to a present climax (*The Cuisine of Sacrifice*, 20 and 224.

[16] J.-M. Oughourlian, *The Puppet of Desire*, 56–59.

only certain inspired works. Shakespeare and Proust, Greek tragedy and Cervantes, saw the GMSM more or less clearly. The Bible presents it lucidly and without fear, to warn us and to turn us to repentance. Beginning with certain inspired passages in the Old Testament, like the judgment of Solomon and the songs of the Suffering Servant, and reaching a climax in the narratives of the passion and the Pauline theology of the cross, the Bible holds before our eyes the lamb slain from the foundation of the world. The central image of the murdered young man draws our attention to the GMSM beneath the surface—of the text, of the culture, and of our own desire.

Girard likes to proceed by comparing texts. For instance, the deception of old Isaac by the ruse of covering Jacob with an animal skin, when compared with the deception of the Cyclops by Odysseus and his men, who escape from the Cyclops' cave by clinging to the bellies of the sheep, shows the trace of the saving power of animal sacrifice. In both cases, the blind master runs his hands over the animal skins and those hiding beneath them are saved. Men escape death by identifying with animals, especially animals killed or to be killed for that purpose.[17] By such comparison, one discerns the traces of the GMSM in the texts.

Girard has described his method as a radical structuralism because the text is generated by something other than the imagination of a Cartesian subject. By "radical" he means that he is neither a structuralist of the usual kind nor a poststructuralist. He is not a poststructuralist for the simple reason that he maintains the obvious notion that texts refer to things other than themselves and that there is a reliable correlation between signifiers and what they signify. The poststructuralist idea that the meaning of a word is given by its difference from other similar words, and that meaning is arbitrary because these differences are, in principle, infinite, is obviously unsatisfactory.[18] The structuralist idea, however, that the structures of a text—its poetics—are generated by the rules of transcendental grammar warrants more attention.

Structuralism is an instance of the triumph of language in the contest to understand the human world.[19] It holds that the forms of linguistic

---

[17] *Violence and the Sacred*, 6.

[18] I am convinced by Terry Eagleton's claim (*Literary Theory*, 142) that poststructuralism was a reaction to the failure of the student revolution of 1968. When the students and their faculty supporters discovered that the communist system was just as oppressive as the capitalist one, they struck at the very notion of system, substituting erotic play for reliable signification. See also J. Culler, *On Deconstruction*.

[19] R. Girard, "Differentiation and Reciprocity in Lévi-Strauss and Contemporary Theory," in *To Double Business Bound*, 155–77.

expression bear the imprint of the common mind. It is, therefore, a transcendental idealism that replaces the ideas of traditional idealism with language. This language (*langue*) is not the actual speech (*parole*) of any group, but the presupposition of the ability to communicate at all. The effect of structuralism is to invest the intellectual dimension of experience with inordinate power. It is the preferred position of intellectuals for whom theory takes precedence over practice. It sometimes claims, unwarrantably I believe, the opening of John's Gospel as its creed: "In the beginning was the word."

Girard's radical structuralism prefers Faust's interpretation of that biblical text: "In the beginning was the deed." Generativity operates primarily in what is done rather than what is thought, in history rather than language. Because it begins from human desire rather than human intellect, the theory of the GMSM is an account of human relations rather than human communication. In the terms of religion, it gives ritual the primacy over myth.

However, action and communication clearly cannot be separated decisively. Some have argued that ritual is itself essentially a communication.[20] Nevertheless, there are advantages to be gained from shifting one's starting point from things thought to things done, from the structure of the mind to the structure of society. It enables one to explain more of the data, and it prevents ethical carelessness. The GMSM explains all of the linguistic phenomena that structuralism highlights, and some, like the fact that the expulsions in the myths are so often violent, that it cannot explain.[21] Furthermore, it accounts for the ubiquity of violence by integrating it into the explanation of the human situation and not treating it as a surprising aberration.

The GMSM, therefore, enables a robustly empirical approach to the understanding of human relations. The data for it are everywhere—in the revenge and scapegoating that drives the world, and in the rituals, myths, and prohibitions that make up the history of religion. It has an immediate affinity for a text centered on the murder of an innocent young man.

---

[20] The definition of ritual given by Konrad Lorenz and accepted by Walter Burkert is a pattern of action that has been detached from its original purpose and is carried on purely for the sake of communication. See W. Burkert, *Homo Necans,* 22–34. Burkert is, however, far from the idealism of classical structuralism. He gives a very helpful, nuanced discussion of the relationship among myth, ritual, language, and communication.

[21] R. Girard, "Violence and Representation in the Mythical Text," in *To Double Business Bound,* 178–98.

This affinity provokes the criticism that the GMSM is simply the imposition of Christian dogma on the world. Girard claims that he came to the Bible by following the trace that he first found in Cervantes, and that the correspondence between the Christian analysis of the human world and the theory of the GMSM is due to the fact that both are empirically correct. The argument has to be settled on the basis of the evidence, and there is a lot of it to sustain the claim of both that violence is not incidental but rather constitutive of the human world, and that religion is both the concealer and the revealer of this fact.

The Gospel in the Gospel

The gospel is a critical interpretation of culture because it discloses the victim. Gospel is the opposite of myth. In the realm of texts, the double transference generates myth. Myth is the narrative version of the lie of the Sacred. It portrays culture as arising from the victim's death and thus makes murder necessary and good. Myth justifies the murderers; gospel vindicates the victim. In order to do this, the Gospel text decodes the double transference because it is generated not by the GMSM but by compassion for the victim. This revelation and truth-telling is the gospel in the Gospels, and generates the opposite of myth.

The Markan text will expound the meaning of the gospel, and so here I shall say only that the gospel tells the truth about the GMSM and offers the kingdom of God as an alternative. As such, it is a call to repent and to turn to the kingdom of God. The kingdom is the power of compassion for victims, structured by the imitation of Christ, especially in his self-sacrifice on the cross. The source of this enlightenment and power is, of course, the God who is beyond our powers to describe, the one to whom the gospel points us as the only possible alternative to the GMSM.

As we shall see in the course of the exposition, the gospel affects but does not change the structures of sacred violence in this world. It opens the possibility of new content for those structures, but leaves the structures intact. For this reason, the poetics of gospel are not exactly correlative with the poetics of violence. The structures of the Sacred and the customs of scapegoating persist but through the disclosure of the gospel we can relate to them differently. The poetics of the gospel enable the withdrawal of acquiescence in the power of violence; thus they deconstruct sacrificial culture without destroying it. Its destruction will come only if and when there is a final transformation.

We shall, therefore, be on the lookout for traces of the GMSM and its opposite in the text. To anticipate our results, the generative process at work in Mark is the opposite of the double transference. It uncovers the founding mechanism that the double transference conceals. The death of Jesus reveals that the victim is innocent and so exposes the founding lie of the order of sacred violence symbolized by the temple. The Cross strips the veil from the Sacred and shows that responsibility for violence lies with the group and not in a fiction. Significance is eccentric, therefore the way of faith leads away from the temple and away from the crowd.

Generative and Thematic Levels

There are two levels to the text: the generative level, where the power that produces the text is located, and the thematic or surface level, where the traces of that generative activity are evident. I use the terms *double transference, founding mechanism,* and *sacred violence* to designate a process at the generative level of the text, which I summarize by the initials GMSM (generative mimetic scapegoating mechanism). On the thematic level, I use *sacrificial system* and other matter-of-fact references to the historical practice of the temple cultus to designate the sacrificial practice that Mark presents as taking place in the temple in Jerusalem. The latter is the thematic expression of the former.

There are different degrees of candor at the thematic level. At one end of the spectrum is myth, where the violent Sacred is concealed; at the other end is gospel, where it is revealed. Two different generative energies correspond to these two types of text. The mechanism that generates myth is the GMSM and the energy that generates Gospel is gospel. Gospel is the opposite of the GMSM as the Gospels are the opposite of myths. In between these limits are the various possibilities of revelation and concealment. "In history we are always between the gospel and myth."[22] The Gospels are also in history, and I hope to show that there is gospel in the dialectic of that travail by reading the Gospel of Mark as an instance of the dialectic of the gospel and the Sacred.

---

[22] Girard, in Hamerton-Kelly, *Violent Origins,* 145.

The Historical Jesus

I do not try to isolate the level of tradition that can be assigned to the historical Jesus, nor to trace the history of that tradition within the Markan sources. The text has been structured by the impact of Jesus on the deep structure of human existence, and this can be discerned without certifying any single event or saying as from the historical Jesus himself. Through the text, one sees the general imprint of his work on human consciousness in his time and ours. The generative energy in the gospel that discloses the GMSM and the possibility of the kingdom of God is the impact of the person of Jesus—through his teaching, death, and resurrection—on the deep structures of human existence, structures formed by the GMSM. The gospel of the kingdom of God works like a leaven on us to uncover the cruelty of the GMSM and to offer the possibility of deliverance from its coils. The historical Jesus is the gospel in the Gospel.

1

Sacred Violence and Sacred Space
Jesus in the Temple (11:1—12:44)

The temple stood as a sign of the need for victims; every day, it offered public and private sacrifice for the good of society. It was the supreme religious and political institution in Judea at the time of Jesus.

It overshadowed Jerusalem and dominated life in the city.[1] Eighty percent of employment in Jerusalem depended on the temple, not only on its day to day ritual needs but also on the periodic pilgrim festivals and the ongoing building project which it constituted. Nine thousand priests and Levites worked there, although not at the same time, operating what was in fact a giant abbatoir. The twice-daily official sacrifices on the vast ever-burning altar consumed thousands of animals and forests of wood. There were cattle pens on the north side and sometimes the water of the Kidron stream where the blood was flushed became so thick that it was sold to farmers as fertilizer. Over it all hung a pall of smoke from burning flesh, and when the great pilgrim festivals, like Passover, were in full swing the priests stood in blood sacrificing the victims of private offerings. Jews were expected to make the pilgrimage to the temple three times a year, twice in the spring—at Passover and Pentecost—and once in the fall, at Succoth. Therefore Jerusalem thrived on what today would be called the convention business. This combination of smoke, blood, and business, whose priests were in league with Roman

---

[1] Evidence comes from the Mishnah and Josephus. For a convenient compendium see J. Jeremias, *Jerusalem in the Time of Jesus,* and E. P. Sanders, *Judaism.*

power to preserve their office and their landed interests, was the historical reality of the sacred for the Gospel of Mark.

Because the power of the Sacred is represented most clearly in religious and political institutions, we have chosen to begin our probe with the pericopes that feature the leaders of those institutions, and the crowd—the symbol of the mob—pursuing the victim (Mark 11–12). Then we shall read the pericopes that tell of the destruction of the temple and the killing of the victim (Mark 13–15), and finally we shall use the insights gained to interpret the poetics of the gospel and the generative mimetic scapegoating mechanism (GMSM; see above) in the rest of the text.

Because the GMSM orders society, we shall refer to its product as an "order." The mechanism of sacred violence produces the order of sacred violence. In the case of the gospel, however, we shall speak of "community" rather than order because "community" describes a society based on the free assent of its members while an order entails deception and coercion.

Furthermore, the structures of the old order persist and the new community emerges within the old order. Thus, the energy of the divine love in the gospel produces the new community of the kingdom of God within the order of sacred violence. The Gospel text presents a vision of a new community generated by a new revelation inspired by the innocent victim who gives his life to found the "kingdom of God."[2]

The Entry of Jesus into the Temple (11:1-11)

Jesus challenges the authority of the order of sacred violence represented by the temple, and Mark narrates the challenge in terms of the conflict between Jesus and the religious, legal, and political representatives of sacred authority. Mark begins the controversy by locating Jesus in the temple, at the center of sacred space.

The point of the pericope is the entry of Jesus into the temple, not his entry into Jerusalem in general.[3] He is the victim coming to the

---

[2] G. W. E. Nickelsburg, "The Genre and Function," argues plausibly that the Markan passion narrative is patterned on a well-attested generic model of a story of the persecution and vindication of a righteous person. Examples from the same tradition as Mark are the Joseph story in Gen 37ff., the story of Ahikar, the book of Esther, Daniel 3 and 6; the story of Susanna; and, with some qualifications, Wis Sol 2:4-5. Nickelsburg begins his characterization of the passion narrative with Mark 11:15-18 in order to make it fit the genre.

[3] D. Juel, *Messiah and Temple,* 127: "From the moment Jesus enters Jerusalem, the story focuses on Jesus and the temple."

place of sacrifice. The statement, "Into Jerusalem into Bethphage" (11:1), links the city and the temple because, according to the Talmud, Bethphage was the outermost limit of the sacred precinct. The consecration of showbread there was valid, up to but not beyond Bethphage[4]. The closing statement, "And he went into Jerusalem into the temple" (11:11), is parallel to 11:1, and summarizes the aim of locating Jesus within sacred space.

The account of the procession has been influenced by Zech 9:9 in a messianic direction—"Behold your king comes to you meek and riding upon an ass"—but it remains predominantly a festal procession into the temple. Palm branches and the cry "Hosanna" (Ps 118) are especially associated with the feast of Tabernacles.[5] Indeed, in the Talmud, the palm branch used at Tabernacles was called the "Hosanna."[6] The use of Ps 118:25-6 in 11:9 foreshadows its use in 12:10-11, where the passage about the rejected stone becoming the head of the corner (Ps 118:22-23) is cited, thus linking Jesus' entry to the temple with his rejection and the building of a new "temple" with him as the cornerstone. This is an instance of the trope known in Greek drama as "foreshadowing."[7]

Thus, the victim is in the temple and is positioned to interact with the sacrificial system in all its manifestations.

The Sacrificial System Is like a Barren Fig Tree (11:12-26)

The key to an understanding of the two incidents narrated here, the attack on the traders in the temple and the cursing of the barren fig tree, is that the one is placed within the other. The attack on the traders is placed within the cursing of the fig tree. This composition warrants our seeing the tree as a symbol of the sacrificial system whose time is now passed ("It was not the season for figs," 11:13). The command, "May no one eat fruit of you ever again" (11:14), is interpreted by the expulsion of the money changers and victim mongers (11:15-16) to mean that the sacrificial system must come to an end. These money changers and victim mongers were essential to the operation of the sacrificial system. They provided the currency and the victims necessary for the offering of

---

[4] H. L. Strack and P. Billerbeck, *Kommentar zum Neuen Testament,* 1: 839.
[5] Cf. the allusion to Tabernacles in the Transfiguration in 9:5. Jesus inherits and transcends the authority of Moses and Elijah and now enters the temple to exercise it.
[6] Strack-Billerbeck, *Kommentar zum Neuen Testament,* 1: 850.
[7] S. H. Smith, "The Role of Jesus' Opponents," 161.

individual sacrifices.[8] In attacking them, Jesus attacks the whole system. Because it does not bear fruit, does not feed the spiritually hungry (11:12), the system must stop.[9]

So this is not a "cleansing" of the temple because unholy trade polluted it, but rather an act of prophetic symbolism foretelling the end of ritual sacrifice. Ed Sanders considers it an act of the historical Jesus; it may indeed have been so, but that is of no importance to our purpose, because the Markan community clearly understood it to authorize and prophesy the destruction of the temple and the inauguration of a new form of piety, the piety of prayer (11:17).

The texts cited from Is 56:7 and Jer 7:11 (11:17) repudiate sacrificial exclusiveness. A community that maintains its unity by scapegoating is inevitably an exclusive and excluding community. This can be seen in the traditional link between initiation and sacrifice. Henri Hubert and Marcel Mauss, Jane Harrison, and Arnold van Gennep regard initiation and sacrifice as the primordial religious rites, and Henri Hubert and Marcel Mauss suggest that the link between the two is the fact that the rules of initiation are originally and essentially those governing entry to and exit from the sacrificial precinct.[10]

The original context of the quotation from Isaiah tells of the admission of foreigners to the cultic community, and the passage from Jeremiah repudiates a superstitious notion that ritual will defend the temple from destruction despite the moral failure of the worshipers. We may also hear in the phrase "a bandits' cave" ($\sigma\pi\acute{\eta}\lambda\alpha\iota\sigma\nu$ $\lambda\eta\sigma\tau\hat{\omega}\nu$) an allusion to the zealot takeover of the temple in the latter days of the Roman war, when it became quite literally a refuge of bandits and a place of open violence.[11] Thus, sacrificial exclusion and fanatical

---

[8] The enigmatic remark that Jesus would not let anyone carry anything in the temple precinct (11:16) does not mean that Jesus is especially concerned for the sanctity of the temple, but rather that he wishes to bring its functioning to a standstill (W. Kelber, *The Kingdom,* 101).

[9] Juel, *Messiah and Temple,* 131, focuses the rejection on the leaders of the temple. We hope to show that they function only as representatives of the system, so that it is the system as a whole and not merely its current leadership that is being rejected, because it represents the mechanism.

[10] D. O'Keefe, *Stolen Lightning,* 167–72; H. Hubert and M. Mauss, *Sacrifice,* 19–49. Walter Burkert (*Homo Necans,* 12) bases his explanation of sacrifice originating as the ritualization of the hunt on Hubert and Mauss's division of the sacrificial process into three parts: the careful approach, the scrupulous departure, bracketing the "deed." Maurice Bloch, (*Prey into Hunter,* 8–45) gives recent evidence of the similarity between initiatory and sacrificial rituals.

[11] M. Borg, *Conflict, Holiness, and Politics,* 174 ($\lambda\eta\sigma\tau\alpha\acute{\iota}$ is Josephus' word for the military opponents of Rome).

violence converge in the allusions to scripture, confirming that the founding mechanism is being disclosed in the narrative.

The temple is a place of violence that shows its nature by the exclusion of the stranger, which is a form of sacrificial victimage. In the original context of the Jeremiah quote, there is a prophecy of the destruction of the temple (Jer 7:12-15), an echo of which we are intended to hear, along with the hint that it is to be replaced by a way open to the stranger who wishes to draw near to God. This complex of ideas recalls the Pauline struggle with the Mosaic law about initiation into the covenant community, and his affirmation of the primacy of faith.[12] The understanding of faith in the text is essentially the same as Paul's.

Faith and Prayer Replace Sacrifice

Sacrifice Is the Same as Vengeance (11:17, 22-25)

The sacrificial system is to be replaced by faith and prayer founded on *the renunciation of vengeance* (11:17, 22-25). Sacrifice is vengeance deflected onto the victim. Originally, vengeance is a form of mimetic violence; it is transformed by the double transference into the vengeance of the god upon those who violate the prohibition. Vengeance is, therefore, integral to the Sacred, and so a renunciation of the Sacred must include the renunciation of revenge.[13] Because vengeance is so close to the heart of the GMSM, the injunction, "Whenever you stand praying, forgive if you have anything against anyone, so that your Father in heaven may forgive you your trespasses" (11:25), is set off in a position of emphasis at the end of the teaching on faith and prayer. If faith and prayer are to replace the sacrificial mechanism, vengeance must be renounced; to renounce vengeance and to break with the GMSM is the same thing.

Thus, the narrative takes us from public to private devotion, from the temple cult to faith and prayer. This recalls Emile Durkheim's theory of the relation between magic and religion. Magic is the appropriation of public religious instrumentalities for private ends. Religious feeling is the individual's awareness of the group, experienced initially in those common activities in which the individual feels swept up and carried

---

[12] R. G. Hamerton-Kelly, "Sacred Violence and the Curse of the Law (Galatians 3:13)."

[13] Cf. S. P. Stetkevych, "Ritual and Sacrificial Elements" and "The Ritha' of Ta'abbata Sharran," for an account of the link among vengeance, sacrifice, and initiation according to the theories of van Gennep and Hubert and Mauss.

beyond self. Religion is the business of the group, or crowd, or mob; magic is the business of the individual. The individual misappropriates these public instrumentalities for private ends in order to help maintain an individual identity within the group.

Faith Is Action as an Individual Apart from the Crowd

Our text puts a remarkable emphasis on the ability of the individual to do for himself or herself what formerly only the system could do. It expresses an extraordinary confidence in the individual and urges an energetic resistance to the group. "Have faith in God. Truly I say to you, whoever says to this mountain, 'Be taken up and cast into the sea,' and does not doubt in his heart but believes that what he says shall come to pass, it shall happen for him. For this reason I say to you, whatever you pray for and seek, believe that you have received it, and it shall be yours" (11:22-24). In the hyperbole of these sayings, the antidote to the power of the group is an individual self-confidence founded on the renunciation of vengeance. This is faith, not magic, and it states a new and potentially liberating end to religion as transfigured violence. The individual, hitherto constituted by mimetic membership in the group—of which vengeance is a prime expression—and nonexistent apart from it, is now to be constituted by "faith in God" (11:22).

In the realm of the Sacred, the individual is constituted by acquisitive and conflictual mimesis as triangular desire mediated through a human model/obstacle. The mimetic subject is constituted within the solidarity of the mob and is the result of a conspiracy to commit murder and to cover up the crime. The emergence of an emphasis on the individual apart from the group should, therefore, be read as a sign of transition from involvement in the mob to membership in the community of the kingdom of God, a change of sides from the executioners to the victims. It is not an endorsement of liberal individualism but a recognition that one has to withdraw oneself from the mimetic power of the mob if one is to enter the loving community, and that such a withdrawal requires resoluteness.

In the loving community, faith constitutes the individual as a different triangle: desire is mediated through the divine, who is too far above to become either a proper model or an actual obstacle. The individual constituted by faith in God is not the metaphysically founded individual of the Aristotelian soul, which would be the basis of a traditional liberal individualism, but the biblical individual created by the word of God and sustained in responsibility to that word. Thus, in a paradoxical sense, the postmodern deconstruction of the individual is affirmed and overcome by the metaphysics of faith, not of presence. The individual exists in a triangular relationship of love that includes the self, the other, and the divine mediator. Here, we encounter for the first time one of the recurring ways in which Mark presents the conflict between the gospel and the Sacred, namely, the dialectic of the individual and the group.

The Crowd and Its Leaders

The representatives of the group come upon the scene at the end of the temple "cleansing" incident.[14] They are separately designated because we are to see Jesus in conflict with every one of the established authorities as they are introduced by name in the course of the narrative. We meet "the chief priests and the scribes" (11:18), that is, the administrative and legal managers of the temple. We also meet that source of all authority, the crowd (ὄχλος) (11:18).[15] We are told that the authorities were afraid of Jesus because the crowd was hypnotized (ἐξεπλήσσετο) by his teaching (11:18). This revealing statement is usually taken to mean that the crowd was on his side; but that is a misunderstanding and it causes a further misunderstanding when later the crowd turns on him. The crowd is not on his side; for the most part, it is on the side of the leaders, and only wavers from time to time in response to Jesus' teaching and miraculous power. Even in its waverings, it remains essentially on the side of the leaders, within the order of sacred violence.

The leaders fear Jesus because his teaching has enthralled the crowd and, for the moment, removed it from their control. It is not positively on Jesus' side but only unavailable at the moment to the temple managers. The term ἐκπλήσσω means, literally, "to strike out, to drive away from, to expel" and here seems to bear the metaphorical meaning of "to strike out of one's senses, to be overwhelmed with desire." The teaching[16] and actions of Jesus have caused the crowd to be overwhelmed with desire, because he has impugned the sacral institution that channels desire. The teaching has expelled them from the womb of

---

[14] J. D. Kingsbury, "The Religious Authorities."

[15] See the section below on the crowd in Mark. Cf. R. A. Horsley, *Jesus and the Spiral of Violence*, 90–120, for an account based on Josephus of the Jerusalem crowd and its political importance.

[16] In Mark, "teaching" refers to "the rule of God and the destruction of evil powers," V. Taylor, *The Gospel according to St. Mark*, 172.

sacred violence and they are on the verge of chaos. No wonder the chief priests and the scribes fear Jesus!

Authority and the Crowd (11:27-33)

All political and social authority derives from the crowd by the double transference.[17] The religious institutions were the original structures of this authority. The Gospel discloses this fact by making violence and authority an ongoing theme, of which this account of a clash between Jesus and the temple authorities is an instance.

Jesus is "walking about in the temple" (11:27) in the style of the peripatetic teacher. The authorities approach him with a question. They are carefully identified as "the chief priests, the scribes, and the elders," thus symbolizing sacred violence in three of its most respectable guises: religion, law, and politics. They ask, "By what kind of authority do you do these things? Or who gave you this authority to do these things?" (11:28). This is the question about the legitimacy of power, about its nature and its source. What kind of authority is it, and who gave it to you?

We assume from the context that "these things" is the attack on the sacrificial system through the hawkers and money changers. The question, therefore, acknowledges that this authority comes from beyond the sacred system. It insinuates that such an attack on the system from which all authority derives threatens chaos. It is the "law and order" argument for political repression, the Grand Inquisitor's reason for religious institutions. Jesus uncovers the bias of the question by asking them in his counter-question to describe the nature of the noninstitutional authority of John the Baptist. They refuse to do so "because they feared the crowd" (ἐφοβοῦντο τὸν ὄχλον, 11:32), which is the source of their own authority. They do not wish to admit that anyone outside their system could be authoritative, especially in the presence of their own source of authority. Such an admission to the crowd would be a betrayal of the conspiracy of the double transference, which must be unanimous to be successful.

---

[17] The word "authority" (ἐξουσία) shows it has been generated by the Sacred by the fact that it can mean both power or authority in the sense of the intrinsic ability and legal right to do something, on the one hand, and the abuse of power in the sense of arrogance and license, on the other. It means both order and its opposite, disorder, just as the primitive Sacred means both succor and threat.

In the counter-question, Jesus limits the options to two mutually exclusive sources of authority: men or heaven. The established leaders do well tactically to refuse to answer on these narrow grounds, because they wish to argue that their authority is both from heaven and from men, the former being mediated through the latter. The crowd, however, has a vague notion of prophetic authority as the authority that comes from heaven.

The Weberian categories of charismatic and institutionalized authority might classify the two types of authority, but they do not explain them. The key to an explanation is that the authority of John is the authority of the expelled victim, as the immediately following parable of the wicked husbandmen indicates (12:1-12), while the authority of the leaders is that of the expellers. John and Jesus are doubles of a different kind than the monstrous doubles of the sacrificial crisis. Their doubling is a doubling of the victim; both are cast out and killed, and both manifest a different kind of power because of that. Their authority is the authority of the scapegoat; it is also the authority from heaven.

On the surface, the dilemma of the leaders is obvious. The crowd took John for a prophet and the leaders killed him. If they admit that he was a prophet, they show themselves to have acted against God; if they deny that he was a prophet, they risk losing credibility in the eyes of the crowd that took him as such. Because their authority rests entirely on the acquiescence of the crowd, they cannot risk antagonizing it, and so they cannot answer the counter-question. Beneath the surface, the admission of any other source of authority would undermine the conjuration of the Sacred and subvert the established order. However, the crowd, which did nothing to prevent them from killing John in the first place, is easily put off by prevarication, and the leaders do not have to answer the counter-question.

The crowd remains, therefore, the explosive but manipulable source of the authority of the powers, and the exchange ends inconclusively. Nevertheless, we have been shown a sort and source of authority other than sacred violence—the authority of the victim. And there is at least a hint that the crowd could take the part of the victim and find the new authority, "from heaven."

The "Crowd" and the Poetics of the Scapegoat

Behind every crowd stands the original lynch mob ready to hound the scapegoat to death. In the Markan drama, the crowd (ὄχλος) or multitude (πλῆθος, 3:7) is a major player whose character undergoes development in the course of the plot. We pick up the crowd as it welcomes Jesus into Jerusalem and into the temple with palm branches and "Hosanna," but by this time it already has a history in the plot, which we should consider before proceeding.

The crowd is the constant background of Jesus' action, even when not specifically mentioned or when the disciples are receiving private instruction. It is the foil for the privacy and the other pole of the insider/outsider structure in the Gospel. It is vaguely analogous to the chorus in Greek drama; it represents common wisdom and comments obtusely on the action. Its role may be summarized in the following categories.

The Crowd Represents All of Israel in Its Quest for Salvation

In going out to John the Baptist or Jesus in search of salvation in the form of healing and teaching (1:5; 3:7; 5:14; 9:14-15) the crowd represents all of Israel. In this role, the crowd shows some wisdom, although in the first part of the narrative we are never clear whether it seeks Jesus for the right reason. As the action progresses, the crowd's motives are shown to be mixed, shallow, and easily manipulated. The crowd seeks salvation, but it does not know what it is looking for and so cannot recognize it when it sees it.

In Its Marveling at Miracles, It Shows the Typical Attitude of the Sacred

It is impressed with raw power and unwilling to see the meaning of the miracles in terms of the disclosure of the identity of Jesus. It is constantly amazed at Jesus' power (1:22; 2:12; 5:20), registering the stock response of common sense to the miraculous. Thus, it signals to the reader like the laugh-track on a sit-com and conveys the same superficial reaction and essential incomprehension.

It Is the Negative Pole of the Poetics of the Scapegoat

It represents the lynch mob in pursuit of the victim. It presses in on Jesus and makes it difficult for him to do his work so that he has to flee from time to time (1:37, 45; 3:9; 3:20; 4:1; 4:36; 5:21, 24; 6:45, 53-56; 8:1; 9:25, 30). It provides the foil against which Jesus is identified as the scapegoat by contrast and differentiation from the group. He and John the Baptist are distinguished from it by clear marks. When Jesus gets into a boat to teach, we are to see the distance he puts between himself and the crowd as significant (4:1).

As the plot progresses, there is a development in the crowd's role as foil and counterpoint to the scapegoat. In the early part of the Gospel, there is a contrast between the crowd and the rulers, shown by the fact that the rulers are introduced without the crowd (3:1-5; 7:1). In the passion narrative, however, the crowd and the rulers merge into a violent mob (14:42, 54-56, 64; 15:6-15, 16, 24). Especially important here is 14:64, which emphasizes that the sentence of death was unanimous. The unanimity of the persecuting mob is a feature of the double transference; that is why the crowd changes into a mob as we approach the actual sacrifice of the victim. There is a foreshadowing of this change of the crowd into a mob in the passion prediction in 9:31, where Jesus is to be "given into the hands of men" in the sense of the mob. The progressive disappearance of differences among the various classes of antagonists—leaders, disciples, crowd— corresponds to the progress of the drama toward the sacrifice.

Even the disciples, who are initially separate from the crowd, disappear into the mob as the narrative progresses. Jesus calls them out (1:16-20; 2:13-17; 3:13-19) and gives them special instruction (4:10-12, 34), but, after the misunderstanding of the passion prediction in 8:31-33, they are ranked with the crowd (8:34) on the side of Satan. Just when they confess the secret and are most inside, they become outsiders again.[18] At last they all forsake him and flee (14:50). This symbolizes the nature of the church as only partly faithful and able to live only by repentance and forgiveness.

In this role, the crowd is fickle; it easily changes sides. It leads Jesus triumphantly into Jerusalem (11:8-10), protects him in controversies with the authorities (11:32; 12:12; 14:2), and hears him gladly when he redefines the nature of the Messiah (12:37).[19] The next time we meet the crowd, however, it has turned into the armed mob out to arrest Jesus (14:42), and then into the whole Sanhedrin and all the false witnesses and police of the trial scene (14:54-56). Then it is the mob, manipulated by the priests and obeyed by Pilate, which cries for Jesus' execution and Barabbas's release (15:6-15),[20] and then it is the cohort that mocks him

---

[18] W. Kelber, "Narrative and Disclosure."

[19] This statement is a summary of all that has gone before in the relationship between Jesus and the crowd, because after this the crowd turns into the lynch mob of rulers and ruled against the victim. R. G. Hamerton-Kelly, "Sacred Violence and the Messiah: The Markan Passion Narrative as a Redefinition of Messianology, in *The Messiah*, (ed. Charlesworth), 461–93.

[20] See Horsley, *Jesus and the Spiral of Violence*, 90–120.

in the praetorium (15:16). Finally, it is the passersby and priests who rail at Jesus on the cross, and his fellow victims who are contemptuous of his messianic dignity (15:24, 29-32).

This inconstancy in the behavior of the crowd indicates that a struggle is going on in the Gospel between the gospel and the GMSM, between disclosure and concealment; but even this dichotomy is not clear. The support of the crowd is compromised by its selfishness and incomprehension, and the opposition of the crowd is mitigated by its manipulation by the leaders. In both cases, therefore, it is subject not to genuine convictions of support or opposition but to the alienated responses that result from the nescience and superficiality of mythic confusion. Because of its confinement in myth, the crowd easily changes from an enthusiastic crowd into a hostile mob when the tide begins to flow against Jesus. The reason for this change is not psychological but generative—part of the poetics of sacred violence. The phenomenology of the crowd is, therefore, essentially the poetics of the GMSM.

It Is Also the Negative Pole of the Poetics of Faith

By token of the scapegoat, those whom Jesus helps have to come out of the crowd (7:53; 8:23; 9:17). *Coming out of the crowd to avail oneself of Jesus' power and then to confess him by standing forth is called faith (5:33-4).* It is identification with the scapegoat. The crowd can come between Jesus and people in need (2:2-4), and the overcoming of this obstacle is also faith (2:5). Unfaith is to remain in the crowd because it is to side with the executioners rather than with the victim. The crowd's unbelief takes the form of solidarity against Jesus; because no one breaks ranks and stands forth to recognize him by asking for help, this solidarity prevents him from working miracles (6:5-6). The crowd is for the most part uncomprehending. It sees but does not perceive, and hears but does not understand (4:12). Only one quarter of it can accept the message of Jesus (4:13-20), and most of it is chiefly interested in miracles (2:12-13; 3:7). It is unable to make up its mind about who Jesus is (6:15; 8:27-30).

Mark Does Not Paint the Crowd in a Uniform Shade of Black; It Is Not the Negative Pole of a Manichean Dichotomy, but Has the Potential to Become the New Community of the Gospel

To have made it a Manichean opposite would have been to repeat the logic of the Sacred rather than to expose it. Rather, Jesus has pity on the crowd because it is without leadership (6:34), and so he teaches it and feeds it (6:33-44; 8:1-10; 10:1). In both feeding stories, the crowd has followed him out into the wilderness and so is in a position where the scapegoat can feed them. For these brief periods, the whole group experiences the nourishment of the community of the scapegoat, even though these are only temporary suspensions of the differentiation between the scapegoat and the crowd. Therefore, the crowd is not endemically and irredeemably evil, and with the right leadership it can transcend the myth of the Sacred and become a community rather than a mob. The gospel is, therefore, not an elitist ideology, and faith is not the same as individualism.

This can be seen in the pericopes where the crowd is transformed into the community around Jesus (3:31-35; 9:33-37). We, the readers of the Gospel, are to see ourselves in the crowd, to identify with the leaderless masses and the uncomprehending disciples, longing for life and truth but manipulated by opportunists of the Sacred. The Gospel tries to alert us to our plight and to call us to stand forth in faith. Once having stood forth alone, however, we are to join the community of the kingdom, the family of Jesus (3:31-35; 9:33-37). The crowd is always potentially a circle of disciples around Jesus, in a community where the lowliest is accepted and respected (9:36).

The Authority from Heaven (12:1-12)

At stake is the relationship between the authority of the crowd/lynch mob and the authority of its victim. Jesus answers the question of authority by means of the parable of the wicked husbandmen, which takes up the theme of the relationship between Jesus and John and carries it forward into the explanation of the new authority. In its reference to John and Jesus, the parable recalls the sayings from Q in Lk 7:33-35 (par. Matt 11:18-19) and in Lk 11:19-51 (par. Matt 23:34-36) that link the two of them together in the chain of the rejected prophets of the divine wisdom.[21] The point of the parable is clear; the religious establishment is opposed to God, and it shows that opposition by killing his representatives. The sacrificial victims are the representatives of God! The issue is defined for us by the preceding question about two kinds of authority, from men and from heaven. The authority from men operates by expelling and killing; the authority from heaven operates by including and vindicating.

---

[21] R. J. Miller, "The Rejection of the Prophets in Q."

The role of Psalm 118 is central to this argument. It was first introduced to herald the entry of Jesus into the temple and announce the coming of the victim to the place of sacrifice (11:9). Here it is invoked to explain the destruction of the temple (12:9) as the vindication of the victim (Ps 118:22-23, quoted in 12:10-11; cf. Acts 4:11; 1 Pet 2:7). The theme of the rejected stone that becomes the head of the corner probably gave rise to the image of the resurrected Christ as the cornerstone of the metaphorical new temple of the Christian community,[22] thus explaining the much discussed "false accusation" in 14:58 that he had threatened to destroy the temple made with hands and replace it in three days with one not made with hands. The whole idea is a metaphor and the "falsehood" of the accusation lodges in the attempt to present a metaphor as a literal threat.

The force of the metaphor is that the sacrificial system of the temple, which symbolizes the GMSM, is replaced by a system that takes its point of departure from the stone that the builders rejected, the victim, and exercises the authority of heaven. The conclusive sign of this new order is the destruction of the temple in the Roman war, an event of recent history of which Mark is vividly aware.

The temple managers perceive that Jesus has told the parable "against" them, and would like to arrest him on the spot, but once again their fear of the crowd inhibits them. Thus, we are brought back as by a refrain to the source of all authority that is "from men," in the crowd. By now it should be clear that the dominant interest of our text is political in the deep sense of the nature and source of the authority that orders human groups. The ground and roots of that authority is mimetic violence running in sacrificial channels. Having dealt with the religious institutions, symbolized by the temple, Mark now proceeds to consider the authority of the state, the law, the Messiah, and the individual, culminating in the vision of the end of all human institutions and modulating into the presentation of the new community based on the death and vindication of the victim.

The Right Attitude toward the State (12:13-17)

Jesus' antagonists from the temple now withdraw and act through representatives. They send to him certain Pharisees and Herodians to trap him

---

[22] Juel, *Messiah and Temple*, 57: "The church is characterized as a spiritual temple made without hands and and is viewed as replacement of the Jewish temple."

into saying something indiscreet and showing himself a revolutionary. The religious antagonists from the temple remain the force behind the opposition, signifying that the GMSM remains the origin of the authority from men no matter what form it takes. The roll of antagonists is lengthened here by the introduction of "some of the Pharisees," carefully designated so as to leave open the possibility that some other members of that persuasion did not oppose him, and the Herodians. The latter are the agents of the Roman puppet king of Galilee and Peraea, Herod Antipas, within whose jurisdiction Jesus as a Galilean fell. The Herodians are the symbol of collaboration with Caesar whereas the Pharisees probably represent the zealous opposition to the Roman rule. The strategy is to trap Jesus one way or another with reference to the two parties represented. If he forbids the paying of taxes he falls afoul of the Herodians and if he advocates it he falls afoul of the Pharisees. In any case, the roll of all the possible representatives of established power is being called and arrayed against Jesus.

They flatter him as part of the stratagem, and with delicious irony they speak the truth. Jesus is, indeed, the one who "is true and does not concern [himself] with anyone nor look upon the face of men but teach[es] the way of God in truth" (12:14). "The way of God" probably includes an allusion to the halakah, which is literally "the way of the law" and the kind of phrase one would expect from the Pharisees, but in the Gospel its primary reference is to the way of Jesus as described in the introduction (1:2-3). The phrase "to regard the face of" is Hebraic (LXX 1 Kgdms 16:7; Ps 81:2; Lev 19:15) and together with the statement that he does not concern himself about any man makes a striking disclosure of precisely what it is that causes men to behave untruly, namely, the concern for others in the sense of the influence of the crowd on the individual.

Daniel O'Keefe[23] presents evidence for "our dizzying susceptibility to one another." Ernest Hilgard argues that hypnotism arises out of our susceptibility to light trances in response to one another. The cognitive dissonance studies of Leon Festinger show that individual perception cannot withstand group influence. The work of Albert Bandura on "modeling" shows that it is impossible not to learn behavior that we see engaged in by others. Girard talks of "mimetic contagion." Here we are told that Jesus does not concern himself with others nor look into the face of another man. Looking into the face of another is the surest way of being entranced by him. Because Jesus does not "look into the face" he

---

[23] O'Keefe, *Stolen Lightning*, 92.

is able to resist mimetic contagion and to be "true." Ironically, the antagonists tell us the secret of his integrity.

Jesus' reply expresses this noninvolvement perfectly. The currency belongs to the state, so let the state have it. The important things belong to God and should be given to God. Jesus refuses to be drawn into either a negative or a positive opposition to the state. If he were to involve himself in such opposition, he would become a part of the violence of either the state or the counter-state, and that would be to succumb to the GMSM. He withholds all cooperation from the mechanism and the result is that rather than Jesus being entranced by his antagonists they are entranced by him (καὶ 'εξεθαύμαζον 'επ 'αὐτῷ, 12:17).

The attitude to the state advocated here is the same as that recommended by Paul in Romans 12:19—13:10, where the apostle, probably in opposition to zealotic tendencies in the congregation,[24] urges the renunciation of vengeance and the acceptance of the established power. The Jewish resistance to Rome that led to the war of 65–70 C.E. is the historical context of the debate about the right attitude toward the state. Jesus and Paul stand aloof from revolution because counter-violence is as much a function of the GMSM as established violence, and one cannot fight the devil with his own weapons. A totally new and different approach is needed, and it begins with taking the part of the victim and refusing all collaboration with violence. But how is this mode of action to succeed? The answer is the vindication of the victim in the resurrection; and so the next challenge is to the concept of resurrection.

The Authority of Love (12:18-44)

Resurrection is the symbol of the new community. It points to a transhistorical, essentially miraculous event. Therefore, the new community of which the Gospel speaks is not the basis for a program of social meliorism in this world, but the ground for a miraculous hope. The historical dimension of the analysis is the exposure of the old order, symbolized by the cross. Conceptually, therefore, resurrection functions as an imagined ideal in terms of which we criticize the actual. The Gospel believed in the possibility of its realization, but, as we shall see from the enigmatic ending of the text (16:8), not in this realm of being.

---

[24] R. Jewett, "The Agitators and the Galatian Congregation"; M. Borg, "A New Context for Romans 13."

"You Are Completely Mistaken!" (12:18-27)

This strong refutation with which the pericope ends shows that something of major importance is at stake. The roll of official opponents is extended once again, this time to include the Sadducees, who deny the possibility of the resurrection of the dead. They are also the priestly aristocracy whose power is the hereditary prestige of the caste that maintains the sacrificial system. We have, therefore, a head-to-head confrontation between a society structured by the Sacred on the one hand, and the possibility of a new society based on the vindication of the victim on the other. This vindication is called resurrection, and the Sadducees seek to ridicule it by an artificial *reductio ad absurdum* based on the law of Levirate marriage.

Jesus refutes these antagonists in their own terms, and this is a new departure. We have just seen how in the questions of authority and taxes to Caesar he bypasses the opponents' terms; the fact that he takes them up here shows that the resurrection is especially important. Other matters might be bypassed, but the resurrection must be established both by Scripture and the power of God. Those who deny the resurrection must be shown to be "completely mistaken," because they deny the possibility of a new community based not on the sacrifice of victims but on their vindication.

Love Is More than Holocausts and Sacrifices (12:28-34)

The religious and the secular powers have been shown to be transcended by the new community of the victim called "resurrection." What then shall be the power of the new community? How shall society be preserved from chaos if not by holocausts and sacrifices? And what shall be the basis of law (prohibition) in the new community?

A lawyer who has been impressed by the astuteness of Jesus' answers asks him for the fundamental principle of the law. Jesus answers with the *Shema,* which is essentially a prohibition on idolatry. The love of God with all one's powers leaves no love for other gods. If there is to be a new community, it must be founded on the renunciation of idolatry, which is the worship of sacrificial violence in the guise of the deified victim. The renunciation of idolatry entails the renunciation of vengeance.

The demand for the renunciation of vengeance takes the positive form of the command to love the neighbor as the self. The full quotation from Lev 19:18 is, "You shall not take vengeance or bear any grudge against the sons of your own people, but you shall love your neighbor as yourself: I am the LORD." It is clearly a proscription of the fundamental principle of law, vengeance. The web of reciprocity must be broken and replaced by a network of love if there is to be a new community, and for that to happen the idol of the primitive Sacred must be forsworn.

Jesus rejects the whole panoply of sacred violence in its first principle as idolatry and its social manifestation as vengeance. The lawyer is the one who expresses this fact when he says, "You spoke elegantly and truly, teacher, when you said that God is one and there is no other besides him, and that to love him with a whole heart and a whole mind and a whole strength and to love the neighbor as oneself is more than holocausts and sacrifices" (12:32-33). Jesus did not speak the words about holocausts and sacrifices; the lawyer added them, and we can only understand them as a summary of all that has gone before in the section beginning with the incident in the temple and the ensuing questioning of Jesus. The lawyer had been listening to the exchanges and was impressed by Jesus' answers. He is not far from the kingdom because he understands the import of Jesus' teaching on the nonsacrificial nature of the new community.

The antagonists are silenced. "No one dared to question him any more" (12:34). It is now clear that a new society called "resurrection" is at hand, based on true transcendence and mutual love, and not on the law of vengeance and the order of the scapegoat. Jesus represents something more than the order of holocausts and sacrifices; he represents a new and different possibility of love. No one dares to question him any longer; now it is his turn to ask the question.

A Different Kind of Messianic Hope (12:35-40)

We are reminded, for the first time since the discussion about authority in 11:27, that Jesus is in the temple. Since we should understand all these debates to have taken place there, the fact that we are explicitly reminded tells us that what follows has special pertinence to the temple.

Psalm 110 testifies that Jesus is not the Davidic Messiah but represents a different messianic hope. The Psalm was widely used in early Christianity (Acts 2:34-35; 1 Cor 15:25; Heb 1:13, 5:6, 10; 7:1, 10-17) to present Jesus as transcending both the political and the priestly messianic hope. The location of this incident in the temple makes it likely that an allusion to the figure of Melchizedek the priest is in the background, and that the text is arguing that Jesus represents a possibility that makes both the religious and the secular political hope obsolete. The letter to the Hebrews spells out the theme of the transcendence of the cultus and the priesthood in terms of the Platonic world of ideas. Here that point is expressed in terms of a new nonsacrificial community in which the violence of the Davidic hope, and the political structure it supports, is transcended.

As David's Lord, Jesus is to bring in a kingdom that is inspired by a different principle than the one that entitles the scribes to the privilege of position, "greetings in the market place, the foremost seats in the synagogue, and the choice places at banquets" (12:39). Such a system devours the weak and encourages hypocrisy. The new community is to be one in which the individual is affirmed. The violent political dreams of the messianic age, measured by the memory of the Davidic kingdom, are replaced by the nonviolent kingdom of the victim vindicated by resurrection.

The crowd seems to be on his side. "The whole crowd heard him gladly" (12:37). What has he said to evoke this positive response from the people? Why should the rejection of the Davidic version of the messianic hope cause such gladness? If we read the text within the context of the war against Rome, we might hear a sigh of relief on the part of those who did not want to be swept up in the violence of an armed resistance inspired by Davidic politics. We might, however, also hear an echo of the old ambivalence about the appropriateness of a monarchical form of government for Israel expressed in the accounts of the establishment of the monarchy in 1 Sam 8-10; and we certainly hear an echo of the humble Messiah of the opening scene who comes to the temple riding on an ass, in step with the prophecy of Zech 9:9, which, although it is not mentioned explicitly by Mark, is in the background and is brought to the fore by the other evangelists.

The monarchy and the priesthood are natural allies and mutually dependent. It was David who first essayed to build the temple, who purchased the threshing floor from Araunah the Jebusite, and who brought the ark to Jerusalem (2 Sam 24:18-25; 6:1-15). It was he who established the system of status based on sacred prestige that excluded the bulk of the populace from positions of power in the state. The message that the common people, the crowd, heard gladly was that this order was to be infused with a new spirit.

The Individual Is Worth More
than the System (12:41-44)

This pericope is an example of the rapacity described in 12:40. The docile contributions of the crowd show that it and the temple are in league.

Then Jesus singles out one person from the crowd, a poor widow who gave her whole life (ὅλον τὸν βίον αὐτῆς, 12:44). She is swallowed up by the temple and its supporting crowd. She is a scapegoat figure. This text is usually read as a moral comment on the relatively greater importance of intention compared to action. Because of the total commitment of the gift, it is worth more than all the other gifts that cost their givers less. But we are left wondering about the fate of the widow, now that she has given her all to the system. How will she live? Is this sort of prodigality really being commended, or are we being shown an example of why the crowd heard with gladness the announcement of the end of the system? We think that the latter message is the more likely, even though the crowd does not understand how the system depends on its complicity. Despite its complicity, the crowd understands the scapegoating method of the temple system.

This story picks up the theme with which the section on the temple began, the theme of the faith of the individual over and against the barren system (11:22-25), and shows how the demands of the system make the life of the individual difficult if not impossible. It tells us that the intention of the individual, misguided and betrayed as it is, is nevertheless worth more than all the crowd's participation in this oppression, and it presents the culminating indictment of the system as it prepares for the climactic announcement of its destruction.

2

Disclosure of the Sacred
The Destruction of the Temple and the Death of Jesus (13:1—16:8)

Not One Stone upon Another (13:1-2)

Now he leaves the temple. The scapegoat goes out and God's presence goes with him. Like Ezekiel (chap. 10) we see God departing from the temple and taking up position "upon the mountain which is on the east side of the city" (Ezek 11:23) as a prelude to the destruction of the city and the departure of its people into exile. We are at a climax of the disclosure of the Sacred and the rejection of the sacrificial system. A disciple draws Jesus' attention to the pretentious size of the buildings, a marvel that impressed Josephus (*Jewish War* 5.189) and can still be appreciated today from the size of the Herodian stones visible *in situ*. Jesus solemnly pronounces the prophecy that not one of these great buildings will remain standing, not one stone remain upon another. The rejection of the Sacred symbolized by the "cleansing" of the temple is confirmed by the prophecy of its destruction, given *ex post facto* by the author of the Gospel. This chapter was written in the light of the Roman destruction of Jerusalem, which was already accomplished.

Signs of Conflict (13:3-36)

Dieter Lührmann[1] sees this discourse as a portrayal in the apocalyptic style of a typical war situation, presenting the position of the Christians caught

---

[1] "Christologie," 67.

35

between the Jews and the Romans in the war of 66–70 C.E. Werner Kelber sees it as an expression of the anti-Zion theology that was "forced upon" Mark by the Roman destruction.[2] We shall follow the main outline of these two interpretations. The war and its aftermath is the context of chapter 13, especially the eschatological hopes aroused by it in the minds of certain Christians. Mark refutes these hopes, especially the idea that the fall of Jerusalem is the eschatological event, and argues that the eschaton is still to come.

The four disciples ask about the time and the significance of the destruction of the temple, and Jesus' speech in answer is a statement of Mark's theology. The speech is organized into three sections and each section has three subsections:

1. A revision of an account of past history, refuting claims that the war is the eschatological event and that the prophets who claimed to be the returning Jesus were in fact he (13:5b-23);

   a. The war (13:5b-8);

   b. Persecution and the Gentile mission (13:9-13);

   c. The "abomination of desolation" and the destruction of Jerusalem (13:14-23).

2. A presentation of the parousia by means of the traditional apocalyptic imagery (13:24-27);

   a. The cosmic drama (13:24-25);

   b. The coming of the Son of Man (13:26);

   c. The gathering of the elect (13:27).

3. A warning of the nearness of the parousia and a demand for constant vigilance because the time of arrival cannot be forecast precisely (13:28-37);

   a. The parable of the fig tree (13:28-29);

   b. Three sayings (13:30-32);

   c. The parable of the doorkeeper.[3]

There are three emphases in the speech: (1) on the need to understand the times properly, (2) on the challenge to endure persecution and

---

[2] W. Kelber, *Kingdom*, 106, 109–28.
[3] Ibid., 126.

maintain watchfulness, and (3) on the duty to carry the gospel to all nations. They amount to an argument that the end of history, while imminent, has not yet come, and that those who say it has are not to be believed. The references to false messiahs and false prophets (13:6, 22) point to rival Christian prophets who misinterpreted the war as the end of the world and the time of the coming of the Son of Man.[4] This is the chief ground for the theory that the passage reflects a controversy within the early church about the meaning of the destruction of the temple in the Roman War. Mark wishes to maintain that the events of the destruction have apocalyptic significance but are not yet the end of the age. They are rather part of the history leading up to the inbreaking of that age—events in the messianic tribulation (13:8c), portending the second coming. As such, they might be called events of apocalyptic history, partaking of the heightened significance of the history that brings the current order of time to an end, but they are history and not eschatology, as Mark's opponents in this argument seemed to have held.

The temple had been a center of resistance during the siege. Several nationalist groups had made it their headquarters and had fought among themselves within the temple walls. The Romans made it the focal point of their siege, and the fall of the temple was tantamount to the fall of the city. The temple was, therefore, the center from which the violence of revolt emanated and to which the violence of repression was directed.

The "abomination of desolation" (13:14) was probably some pagan symbol set up in the temple—an altar, or the standards of the legions. Josephus tells us that the Romans set up their standards in the temple court opposite the eastern gate and, while the sanctuary was burning, offered sacrifices to them, hailing Titus as autocrat (*War* 6.316). On the other hand, because the "abomination" is said to be "standing where it ought not," it might refer to the dramatic epiphany of the Zealot leader Simon bar Giora who had been hiding in the catacombs and whose surrender Josephus describes as follows:

> Thereupon, Simon, imagining that he could cheat the Romans by creating a scare, dressed himself in white tunics and buckling over them a purple mantle arose out of the ground at the very spot whereon the temple formerly stood. The spectators were at first aghast and remained motionless; but afterwards they approached nearer and inquired who he was. [*War* 7.29-30][5]

---

[4] D. Lührmann, "Christologie," 467.
[5] Quoted by J. D. Crossan, *The Historical Jesus*, 205.

Dominic Crossan conjectures that Simon was presenting himself as king of the Jews. If this were so, it would be a counterpart to an earlier, non-violent king of the Jews who had died at the hands of the Romans without bringing the city down with him. Kelber points out that the "abomination" is construed as a person, the masculine participle ἑστηκότα giving a personal identity to the neuter βδέλυγμα (13:14), and this suggests a scenario like the appearance of Simon rather than the impersonal presence of the standards.

In any case, whatever it was, the "abomination" is a sign that disqualifies the temple as the place of the second coming of Christ. Violence is personified, Satan has taken over the temple, and thus it is disqualified forever as the place of the parousia.[6] Accordingly, Mark argues—against the group that holds that the parousia will happen in the temple—that the second coming will be in Galilee (16:7). Could this Jerusalem-centered group have shared the notion, possibly held by Simon bar Giora, that the epiphany of the Messiah in the temple would miraculously reverse the defeat and bring the kingdom of God instead of the empire of Rome? Mark rejects this and similar notions.

The presence of Satan (= the "abomination") in the temple (cf. 8:33) is an unveiling of the violence that has always been its life. The negative apocalypse that reaches its climax here has been coming from the moment when Jesus entered the temple. The "abomination" is not only a historical reference to the Roman and Zealot desecration and a polemical symbol in the argument between two parties in the church but also an unveiling of the GMSM that drives the temple. The temple was the focal point of the resistance to the Roman siege. Rival groups of Jewish nationalists fought each other for possession of it. It was in fact a center of religio-nationalist violence, and Mark interprets that to mean the place of Satan. In Girardian terms, Satan is the mythological symbol of mimetic rivalry, the "abomination" of violent desire.[7] There is a deep consistency, therefore, in the violent Roman destruction of a violent system.

There is also a consistency in Mark's presentation of this apocalyptic speech at this point in the Gospel. It is both a climax to the preceding narrative of Jesus in conflict with the powers of sacred violence symbolized

---

[6] Kelber, *Kingdom,* 119–20. "The ἐρημώσεως was fulfilled in its most radical, literal sense, and the βδέλυγμα was impersonated by Satan himself. Satan had taken possession of the holy temple" (p. 120).

[7] René Girard made this point on the symbol of Satan in the Gospels, in an address to a plenary session of the AAR in San Francisco in November, 1992, entitled, "How Can Satan Cast Out Satan?"

by the religious and secular authorities who confront him in the temple and an introduction to the subsequent narrative of the decisive outbreak of that violence against his person. Werner Kelber explains the positioning of chapter 13 by means of the historical circumstances of the conflict between the Galilean and the Jerusalemite Christian communities; the speech is the climax of the argument made by the former against the position of the latter. This may, indeed, be a part of the explanation for its occurrence here; but it can only be a part of the explanation, because it does not account for the close linkage of this passage with what comes in the succeeding chapters. The "abomination" summarizes the preceding narrative and foreshadows the Satanic violence that will soon break out from the temple against Jesus, the innocent victim. It also alerts us to the other elements in the discourse that foreshadow the narrative to come.

What the reader must understand (13:14) is that the "abomination" is the disclosure of the mechanism of the Sacred and a foreshadowing of the violence that is to come when "the chief priests, and the scribes sought to take him by stealth and kill him" (14:1). This is confirmed by the exhortations to watchfulness in the conclusion of the speech. They point to the Gethsemane scene where the Lord finds the disciples sleeping (13:36; cf. 14:37-41) and utters the same warnings to stay awake and watch (13:33). It is also confirmed by the mention of the crowing of the cock ('αλεκτοροφωνία, 13:35; cf. 'αλέκτωρ 'εφώνησεν, 14:72; cf. 14:30), which recalls the same element in the account of Peter's denial. The frequent references to being "handed over" or betrayed (παραδίδωμι, 13:9, 11-12) recall the betrayal of Jesus and especially the handing over of the Son of Man at the conclusion of the Gethsemane pericope (14:41), which takes place as the disciples sleep. Finally, the threefold organization of the speech recalls the three times Jesus comes and finds the disciples sleeping in Gethsemane, and the three denials of Peter.[8] All of these foreshadowings help the reader to understand that the revelation of the "abomination" is the unveiling of the GMSM that is about to break out against Jesus; it is the clue to the GMSM that generates the action and from now on is to become even more evident. Chapter 13 is, therefore, not merely the climax of what has gone before but also an introduction to what is to come.[9]

---

[8] On Mark's use of a triadal pattern of composition, see G. W. E. Nickelsburg, "Genre and Function," 177–78, and N. R. Petersen, "The Composition of Mark 4:1—8:26."

[9] E. S. Malbon, *Narrative Space,* 151. She cites Norman Perrin and John Donahue to the effect that chap. 13 and chaps. 14—16 are two endings to the Gospel. Donahue characterizes them as the passion of the community and the passion of Jesus respectively.

The role of the section on the parousia (13:24-27) in this chapter is
analogous to the role that the question about the resurrection plays in the
discourses in the temple (12:18-27). It introduces the note of miraculous
intervention and signals that the fulfillment of the hope for a new order
can only take place through the action of God. It is as if for a moment the
veil is lifted and we are shown the real agent in the history that is being
recounted. The temple is to be replaced not with another sacrificial system but with the community of those chosen by the Son of Man, which
in Daniel 7 symbolizes the truly human one,[10] who with the restoration
of the right order of creation takes the place of the beasts as the ruler of
humanity. Sin caused the beasts to rule over Adam in contradiction to
the intended order of creation. Now the right order is restored and the
human one rules in the human community.

It is remarkable that among all the apocalyptic imagery of this discourse there is not one claim that the tribulations to befall humanity
in the messianic apocalyptic history and the ultimate eschaton are ex-
pressions of the vengeance of God. Rather, the suffering is to be caused
by wars, frauds, charlatans, natural catastrophes, misunderstandings, and
persecutions. These are the sadly predictable human failings that cause
human misery without any divine intervention. In fact, the one clear
reference to divine intervention has God shortening the tribulation for
the sake of his elect. There is, therefore, a significant omission of the
divine vengeance from a traditional apocalyptically styled passage, and
that confirms our thesis that the generative energy of the Gospel is the
opposite of the Sacred. Even though traditional imagery is used, the traditional content has been modified so as to remove the idea of the divine
wrath and vengeance. The wrath is the suffering we inflict on ourselves
and each other within the order of the GMSM.[11]

Jesus as Scapegoat (14:1—16:8)

The passion narrative, by completing the identification of Jesus as the
sacrificial victim of the authorities and powers, identifies him as a scapegoat of the GMSM. This is the climax of the disclosure of the Sacred in
the Gospel. The unanimity of the Jewish and Roman powers against the
victim, the peculiar doubling of Jesus and Peter and Jesus and Barabbas,

---

[10] M. D. Hooker, *The Son of Man in Mark,* 15–17.
[11] For the same theme in Paul, see R. G. Hamerton-Kelly, *Sacred Violence,* 101–2,
151–52.

which distinguishes them rather than makes them similar, the incomprehension of the disciples, and the killing of the victim, are all features of the sacrificial crisis and its solution by unanimous scapegoating. The passion narrative is the touchstone of our interpretation.

Burton Mack believes that the Girardian reading of the passion narrative is disingenuous.[12] He argues that it is not a revelation of the GMSM but rather a product of it—the passion narrative reveals just enough of the GMSM to disarm the reader in the process of scapegoating the Jews. It is a myth of innocence that grew up during the conflict between the church and the synagogue over ownership of Israel's religious heritage. It is therefore the result of mimetic rivalry and scapegoating, a myth in the special Girardian sense.

This is an obvious ploy, and Mack makes it with skill and erudition. I do not want to counter it directly; I prefer to continue the interpretation by means of the GMSM and leave it to the reader to decide whether we have here a myth of innocence or the truth of the gospel. The chief difference between our readings is that mine is generative and Mack's is thematic. I look for traces of the GMSM while he looks for historical parallels. I have serious reservations about this comparative historical method and great confidence in the generative method. I believe it provides a convincing reading that is not mythically anti-Jewish.

At the outset, however, I might observe that the mob that kills the victim is indiscriminately Jew and Gentile because of the loss of differentiation in the sacrificial crisis. Pilate, the priests, and the people are indistinguishable in the lynch mob. The disappearance of the principles of discrimination is attested by the release of Barabbas, a real bandit, while Jesus the innocent is executed on a charge of banditry.

Mack holds that Jesus was not innocent, that his condemnation was just, and that the Gospel invented the innocent victim in order to invent the guilty Jews. It is all a construction of political malice worthy of the Balkans. On the level of comparative history, however, we do not have the sources to evaluate such a reconstruction. It is just as likely that a power structure of collaborators and colonialists would execute an innocent "trouble-maker" on trumped-up charges. That the passion narratives were read at later times as texts justifying persecution of the Jews tells us not about the Gospels so much as about the enthrallment of those subsequent readers to the scapegoating myth.

---

[12] B. Mack, "The Innocent Transgressor."

The list of the opponents of Jesus in this section is a roll call of the Jewish and Roman leadership: the chief priests, the scribes, the elders, the Pharisees, the Herodians, the Sadducees, the Romans, and—always in the background—the crowd. The opposition between Jesus and these powers is motivated not by the fact that they are Jews, but that they are the powers of this world. At issue is not the inadequacy of the Jewish religion by comparison with the new Christian religion but rather the violence of the scapegoating order generated by the GMSM and the possibility of liberation from it.

The Priests Buy a Victim (14:1-11)

At several points in the narrative, the powers have indicated a desire to apprehend Jesus; now they fulfill that desire. The temple authorities take the lead again as they did at the beginning of the previous section, after the driving out of the traders. "The chief priests and the scribes sought to take him by stealth and kill him," but once again they are inhibited by the mob (14:1-2). Everything must appear to be done in accordance with the law or out of sight of the crowd lest the authorities lose credibility by disclosing the violence to its source in the mob.

A vignette announces Jesus' impending death (14:3-9), and then we are told how the chief priests arrange with Judas to have Jesus betrayed to them. They promise to give him money, but they do not pay him on the spot.

Money is a continuing theme and a trace of the GMSM. The one who attacked the money changers and the victim mongers is about to be bought as a victim himself. Jesus came to the hostile attention of the powers by driving the money changers from the temple (11:15-19); the issue of his relation to the state was posed in terms of money, and an actual coin was part of the narrative (12:13-17); the throng and the widow acknowledged their thrall to the system by casting money into the temple treasury (12:41-44); and now the chief priests offer money in return for his life. Money as a substitute is a sign of the scapegoat.

As we have argued in the Introduction, money is a powerful symbol of the value of life and plays an essential role in the sacrificial system. We are told, for example, that the widow casts her whole life (ὅλον τὸν βίον αὐτῆς, 12:44) into the temple treasury. The power of money derives from the sacrificial origins of symbolism, rooted in the discovery that one thing, the victim, can substitute or stand for another, the group. The sacrificial victim is essentially a form of currency substituting for the life of the offerer.[13] By taking their money, Judas indicates that he sees Jesus as another victim of the sacrificial system to be killed behind a screen of substitution. The money is the sacrificial equivalent of the life of Jesus[14] and a trace of the GMSM scapegoating its victim.

The Inversion of Sacrifice (14:12-26)

The pericope of the last supper is a narrative counterpart to the account of Jesus' activity in the temple given in chapters 11–12, and the room in which the supper is held is the symbolic counterpart of the temple. The beginning of the pericope recalls the entry into the temple in chapter 11. The same mystery attends the locating of the appropriate room as attended the finding of the ass for the triumphal entry. Disciples are sent on ahead to meet a man marked by the fact that he is carrying a jar of water, which is unusual in a society in which water is usually carried by women. Once in the room, the talk turns to the "handing over" of Jesus as a sacrificial victim to the chief priests, who, like the patrons of the temple traders, have bought but not yet paid for him. (They have merely promised to pay for him, 14:11.)

Judas is the offerer of sacrifice and the servant of the GMSM. The term παραδίδωμι (14:18, cf. 14:11), which in general means simply

---

[13] E. Gans, *The End of Culture*, 34, who proposes an explanation of the origin of culture formally similar to Girard's, although with significant differences, makes the system of exchange that begins with the sharing of the desired object among the participants in what he calls the "originary scene of designation," the central ethical, and therefore constitutive, act of culture. Money originates in this primal sharing of the victim; cf. B. Laum, *Heiliges Geld;* W. Desmonde, *Magic, Myth and Money,* and, for a more general treatment of the role of the sacrificial mechanism in economics, P. Dumouchel and J.-P. Dupuy, *L'Enfer des Choses.*

[14] Matthew makes more of this fact than Mark does, actually calling it "blood money" (Matt 27:6), and treating it as polluted and hence unworthy of being returned to the temple treasury. It is polluted because it represents the scapegoat who must be driven out and not allowed to return. Matthew also puts the incident in the context of a prophecy from Zechariah (Matt 27:9-10 = Zech 11:12-13), in which the money was cast into the temple treasury, in order to make the point of its not being deposited in this case more poignant by contrast. In any case, in Matthew, to return it to the treasury would pollute the temple by interfering with the logic of sacrifice. An offering has been made, a victim/ scapegoat purchased and slaughtered/expelled; to take back the price of the sacrifice would be to contradict the logic of the sacrifice by returning to the temple the violence that the sacrifice/scapegoat bears away. So, instead of returning the money to the treasury, they bought with it a field for the burial of foreigners. The reference to foreigners underlines the scapegoat associations of the transaction; the foreigner, the stranger, is the typical scapegoat. To take back the money would be to take back the scapegoat and so return the violence that they had sought to expel.

"to hand over," takes on the meaning, in this context, of the handing over of a victim, because the recipients are the priests. There is some precedent for this usage in the literature on martyrdom, and in Eph 5:25 we find precisely such a meaning. In Mark, it is used in the predictions of the passion (9:31; 10:33) and of persecution (13:9, 11, 12), and at the conclusion of the Gethsemane scene (14:41). More importantly for present purposes, it appears in the narrative of the handing over of Jesus by the Sanhedrin to Pilate (15:1, 10) and by Pilate to the soldier-executioners (15:15). Judas hands over Jesus as an offerer hands over a victim.

The institution of the Eucharist is an inversion of the temple sacrifices. The usual direction of the sacrificial offering is reversed; instead of the worshiper giving to the god, the god is giving to the worshiper. Jesus "gives" (δίδωμι) his body and blood, symbolized by bread and wine, to them instead of their giving their bodies and blood, symbolized by money, to the temple. Just as money symbolizes life given to the temple, so bread and wine symbolize the divine life given to the worshiper. Bruce Chilton suggests plausibly that the words of institution, "This is my body. . . . This is my blood" (14:22-24) intend to present the breaking of the bread and the pouring of the wine as substitutes for the killing of victims in the temple. The room substitutes for the temple, the table for the altar, and the sharing of the food for the killing of the victim.[15] Normally, the worshiper brings the offering into sacred space; here, the upper room is the nonsacred counterpart of the holy of holies, and so the offering is made outside of sacred space. Thus, the sacrificial system is subverted by the reversal of the direction of its ritual logic.

Judas is traditionally the great gospel scapegoat, but this tradition should be reconsidered. The first thing to note is that there is ultimately no difference between him and the other disciples, because all forsake Jesus.[16] Judas and Peter are in fact doubles; they both betray Jesus. This solidarity of the disciples in opposition to Jesus is skillfully presented in the narrative. Jesus refers to the fact that there is a traitor in their midst but does not name him. This causes the disciples to ask one-by-one, "Is it I?" to which Jesus replies enigmatically. He does not exonerate any of them but states in general terms that it is one of the Twelve who are

---

[15] B. Chilton, *The Temple of Jesus,* 152–53.
[16] I was alerted to this theme by my student, Jerry Feliciano, and I include it here with his permission. The development of it is my own.

sharing the meal with him, someone "who is dipping into the dish with me?" (14:18-21). This in effect means all of them because all share the dish with him, and that is how it turns out, because all betray him in the end.

Judas is not marked as the scapegoat by Jesus, and the traitor is not expelled. Each disciple indicates by his questioning that he is not sure of his own loyalty. Thus Mark indicates that none of us can escape responsibility for the death of Jesus by scapegoating Judas.

The enigmatic "Because the Son of Man goes as it was written of him, but woe unto that man by whom the Son of Man is betrayed. It is better for him if that man had not been born" (14:21) raises the question of election and predestination. Have the disciples in general and Judas in particular been chosen by God to perform the dark deed of betrayal because it is necessary for the divine plan of salvation? Paul understands the role of Pharaoh in the Exodus in this way. God hardened Pharaoh's heart to resist the divine demand so that because of his resistance God would have the opportunity to do spectacular deeds and so spread his fame to the world (Rom 9:17-18).[17] Does Mark have the same theory in mind when he talks of the Son of Man going "as it was written of him?"

The paradoxicality of the sentence shows how it should be read. The unfolding of the career of Jesus towards its culmination in death corresponds to what the scriptures understand to be the typical fate of the servants of God. Those who persecute God's servants act freely and suffer the consequences of their deed. There is, therefore, no need to read it in the Pauline way to indicate a prevenient divine control of events. Other uses of the phrase "it is written" in Mark (1:2; 7:6; 9:12-13; 11:17; 14:27) do, however, suggest a notion of prevenient control, but there is a looseness in the fit between the scriptures cited and the events referred to that suggests a general rather than specific correlation between prophecy and fulfillment. Indeed, some correlations, like 14:27 are like poetic allusions rather than tight prophecies.

In any case, I do not wish to burden my text here with a discussion that might do justice to the thorny problems of election and predestination. There is an important exegetical and systematic reconsideration of these topics waiting to be done.[18]

---

[17] Hamerton-Kelly, *Sacred Violence*, 120–39.
[18] Ibid., 138–39.

The Disciples Succumb to Mimetic Rivalry (14:27-31)

The theme of mimetic rivalry is central in the foretelling of Peter's denial (14:27-31).[19] Jesus warns the disciples that they will all be scandalized (σκανδαλισθήσεσθε) over him (14:27), and interprets "scandal" to mean that they will all be scattered like sheep without a shepherd. The analysis of the meaning of "scandal" in the Gospels belongs among René Girard's most brilliant achievements. Scandal is the hold that the model/obstacle has on desire.

> In the Gospels, the skandalon . . . is always someone else, or it is myself to the extent that I am alienated from other people. . . . Scandal invariably involves an obsessional obstacle, raised up by mimetic desire with all its empty ambitions and ridiculous antagonisms. . . . It is the model exerting its special form of temptation, *causing attraction to the extent that it is an obstacle and forming an obstacle to the extent that it can attract.* The skandalon is the obstacle/model of mimetic rivalry; *it is the model in so far as he works counter to the undertakings of the disciple, and so becomes for him an inexhaustible source of morbid fascination.*[20] [Emphasis added.]

Scandal is an essential feature of what Girard and his collaborators call interdividual psychology.[21] This psychology is based on the rivalry that develops in the mimetic relationship as the imitator becomes like the model and contests the model's access to the object. Both parties then become model and obstacle to each other. The model attracts and obstructs, and the imitator cannot break the relationship because of the power of mimetic desire. They are locked in contradiction, loving and hating each other at the same time.

In Mark, "scandal" means the same as Satan. In 8:32-33, Peter objects to the prediction of the passion and Jesus rebukes him as Satan for thinking "as men think and not as God thinks,"[22] inasmuch as he wants to divert Jesus from the way of the cross. There Peter threatens to become a scandal to Jesus and here Jesus says he will be a scandal to all the disciples. Scandal, therefore, has something to do with the death of Jesus.

Scandal is the inability to affirm the way of the cross or to break the relationship with Jesus altogether. It wants Jesus to use rather than to

---

[19] Girard has treated this incident in *The Scapegoat*, 149–64.
[20] Girard, *Things Hidden*, 416.
[21] J.-M. Oughourlian, *The Puppet of Desire.*
[22] Matthew (16:23) introduces the term "scandal" into this context as the equivalent of Satan, showing that Satan is the mythological representation of mimetic rivalry. This is another instance of Matthew's making explicit what is only implicit in Mark.

suffer sacred violence, to be a hero rather than a victim. The result of the scandal is, therefore, that the disciples wander from the way of the cross and are scattered like sheep without a shepherd (14:27). They are confused and without direction. Unable to take the way of the cross and unable to turn back, they mill around in confusion.

Peter stands for all the disciples and for all the readers of the Gospel as he plays out the scandal before our eyes. He shows that we are enmeshed in sacral categories and want our model to be a greater warrior and a more sacred god than those of others. He shows that we need to be "put down" by our model because that is the way he assures us that he is worthy of our devotion.

So Peter boasts that he will not be scandalized, unaware that the GMSM works best through self-deception. Even after Jesus predicts his denial, Peter refuses to be humble, but in effect makes a liar of the Lord by assuring him, "'Even if I must die with you I shall not betray you!' And thus they all said" (14:31).

Peter has incited the mimetic rivalry of the group by setting himself apart, claiming to be the only one who will not be scandalized. They all imitate him; every disciple regards himself as the exception, the one who will not be coerced by mimetic rivalry. Thus it appears that the very denial of mimesis is mimetic, and so what hope have they of escaping its hold? "Even if I should die with thee, I will not betray thee," says Peter "with great insistence. And thus also said they all" (14:31). "And they all forsook him and fled" (14:50).

Girard's analysis of this passage is marvelously subtle.[23] The enthusiasm of the disciples for sharing the fate of Jesus, the "false eagerness for the Passion" is a satire of "a certain religious fervor which must be recognized as specifically 'Christian.'" The disciples merely exchange the ideology of success for that of suffering and failure, and invent the new religious language of the passion; but both attitudes are driven by the same mimetic mechanism. The latter is no less full of envy and scandal than the former. This means that "[a]ll the forms of adherence that men in groups can give to an enterprise are declared unworthy of Jesus. . . . Christian inspiration at its greatest has no connection with its psychological and sociological by-products."

The point the Gospel makes here is very difficult to grasp for a Christianity that has sold out to secularism. Pathetic Christianity, so

---

[23] *The Scapegoat*, 159.

eager to be of service in the world, sells itself as solidarity with victims for the sake of Jesus, or a way to psychological "meaning" through identification with the crucified. "Even if I must die with you I shall not forsake you." And so say all of us; but the Gospel exposes the fallacy of such spiritual heroics. Not one of those heroes stood by Jesus.

Peter's refusal to believe the Lord's prediction of his failure is the essence of the spiritual pride that would make of the self the great exception. It is better to believe the Lord's prediction, to accept that we are enmeshed in mimetic scandal, and to trust the promise that "After my resurrection I shall go before you into Galilee" (14:28). Only the return of divine grace to lead the scattered flock on the way of resurrection can deliver us from the double-bind of mimetic scandal. The attempt to exalt oneself above the crowd only intensifies its power.

Here the Gospel presents nothing less than the possibility of a relation with God by grace and faith alone. Such faith begins not with the spiritual self-promotion of a pledge of loyalty unto death, but with the humble acceptance of the scandalous self. Such faith is best expressed in the prayer of the publican in Luke 18:13: "But the tax collector standing afar off would not even lift his eyes to heaven, but beat his breast, saying, 'O God, have mercy upon me a sinner.'" Peter's betrayal takes place not when he denies knowing Jesus but when he denies being subject to the power of the GMSM. At that point, he draws all the other disciples into a similar denial and makes them fair game for the GMSM. His piety negates the power of Jesus' warning and interferes with Jesus' work for their souls.

Jesus' impending death, unadorned by the pretense that it is a good thing, will remove him as a sacred object and subvert the possibility of Jesusolatry. That is why Peter protests in 8:32-33 against the fact that Jesus should die at all, and here against the notion that he should die forsaken by all his followers. In order for Jesus to remain a sacred hero, his death must be heroic—either in its courage or in its suffering—rather than ignominious, and his followers should stand fast to the end, showing either great courage or a perfect willingness to suffer. In this way, his death would qualify as a sacrifice or a noble death for the sake of a higher morality or patrician community, and that community would come into being properly, by loyalty and self-sacrifice. Instead, Jesus dies ignominiously and his community humiliates itself by cowardice. Instead of sacred prestige, we have the scandal of mimetic rivalry, and the possibility of a cult of the exultation or a cult of the passion is removed. The Gospel gives us only one option, the simple possibility of grace and faith.

In his discussion of this passage, Girard also makes a novel contribution to the debate about the importance of the Jesus of history. He questions whether "the authors of the Gospels fully understood the scope of this [mimetic] desire which is revealed in their texts."[24] The mysterious reference to the crowing of the cock suggests that Jesus has miraculous foresight, whereas not divine foresight but only human insight is needed to see that the mimetic rivalry expressed in Peter's boast is bound to lead to catastrophe, because it incites the mimetic desire of others. The fact that the text presents this insight as a miracle shows that, at one level, it still does not understand the GMSM. The category of the miraculous, at least in this context, functions as a myth to hide the human source of the action. Mark understands the outcome, but not the process, which remains for him a miracle and myth-representation of sacred violence. Girard suggests that we have here a trace of the difference in understanding between the writer of the text and the luminous intelligence that inspired it, that is, a trace of the historical Jesus, and an indication of how his interpreters failed to understand him fully. Historically, Jesus simply warned Peter about the dangers of mimetic rivalry leading to disloyalty; literarily, Mark turned this warning into a miracle of foresight, and this tendency to invent miracles is an indication of the mythifying operation of the GMSM. Nevertheless, we can see the GMSM through the text and therefore Mark was faithful to the tradition of Jesus, in whose teaching it was revealed even when Mark did not fully understand it.

As the attack on the traders in the temple is set within the account of the cursing of the fig tree and the teaching on faith and forgiveness (11:12-25), so the incidents in Gethsemane and the hearing before the high priest are set within the account of Peter's denial. The account of the denial begins here with the prediction of scandal (14:27-31) and ends with the fulfillment of the prediction in 14:66-72.

The incidents in Gethsemane and the trial before the high priests are, therefore, part of the exposition of what it means to be scandalized by Jesus. In addition to what we have already said, scandal means being unable to give Jesus the moral support he needs (14:32-42), fleeing after his arrest (14:50), and following Jesus to his trial "from a distance" (14:54). Peter's following from a distance is a good example of being in scandal, unable to follow closely and unable to break away. Peter sets himself up for failure.

Gethsemane: The Sleeping Disciples (14:32-42)

The incident ends with all the disciples swearing that they will be true until death (14:31). In the very next scene, they show that they cannot

---

[24] Ibid.

even watch with him as he prays in Gethsemane. They have not understood that Jesus is no sacred hero, religious virtuoso, or saint, but simply
a victim of violence in need of moral support. They fail to understand
that he needs companionship in his time of temptation. Confident that
the great leader has everything under control, they doze off in the midst
of his struggle. They cannot bear to hear that his soul is sorrowful, or
accept his frailty, or believe that he needs their presence and support.
"My soul is very sorrowful unto death" (14:34) is the last thing they
want to hear from him. So they maintain their sacred illusion by shut-
ting out reality in sleep.

The theme of the sleeping disciples is emphasized by being narrated
three times. The first time, Jesus directs his rebuke at Peter for not being
strong enough to stay awake to all that is going on. He warns Peter to be
alert and on guard against temptation, as if he were answering Peter's
declaration of faithfulness unto death in 14:29-31. We are not told what
the content of the second rebuke was, but only that the disciples were
unable to answer him because they were ashamed for not having heeded
the first rebuke. They are ashamed because they do not have the courage
to go through the ordeal with their eyes open. They are ashamed because they have boasted of their loyalty.

The third and concluding comment on their sleep is enigmatic and
plagued by textual uncertainty. We do not know whether it is a question
or a command; we do not know whether to read τὸ τέλος after ἀπέχει in
14:41, and we do not know precisely how to take ἀπέχει. The textual
evidence does not seem to us to favor the inclusion of τὸ τέλος, and the
most likely meaning for ἀπέχει seems to be the commercial one known
from the papyri: "He has been paid." If we take the verse as a command
and not a question, we may read Jesus' third statement as follows: "Stay
asleep for the rest of the time [i.e., for the rest of the drama about to be
played out], and take your rest. He [Judas] has [now] been paid. The hour
has come, behold the Son of Man is handed over into the hands of sinners." The weary and biting irony of "Stay asleep for the rest of the time"
says that we are not able to stand the truth about the founding mechanism
and would rather not be present at its uncovering. We do not want to
know that Jesus is not a hero full of the power to avenge, but rather commands a nonviolent, nonvengeful power that works more subtly.

The fact that the saying is immediately followed by the urgent and contradictory, "Get up! Let's go! See, my betrayer is near!" (14:42) confirms
that we are intended to read the ironic command to sleep on as a metaphor.
"Sleep on for the rest of the time" means, therefore, "You do not have
the strength to go through this with your eyes open, so you might as well

remain asleep." We, the readers, are expected to hear the irony and be convicted by it, and thus motivated to "Stay awake and watch!" so as to see the truth unfold in the text and in the world.

A sequence of action that begins with Jesus telling the disciples that they will all be scandalized (σκανδαλισθήσεσθε, 14:27) by him—in the sense that they will be able neither to support him nor to reject him, but will be bound to him in a bond of morbid fascination—ends with the irony of their sleeping through the revelation of the scandal of mimetic rivalry and surrogate victimage.

All the important action takes place while they (we) dream of a heroic denouement in which violence overcomes violence, Beelzebub drives out Beelzebub, and the scandal of the sacred hero establishes itself . as the truth of religion. In the world of reality, however, the finger of God is driving out violence, in the shape of the unheroic victim of a commercial transaction. He has been bought, and now he has been paid for, and the one who attacked the animal-hawkers has become just one more of their bought-and-paid-for goats. Jesus ends their conspiracy not only by the whip of his prophetic anger, but also by exposing their violent complicity in victims; he destroys the temple made with (blood-stained) hands, and founds the metaphoric new temple not made with hands. His disciples (we, the readers), however, sleep through it all and awake refreshed, with renewed enthusiasm for rebuilding the order that he has just undermined, by idolizing Jesus and installing him in the place of honor in a new temple made with hands.

The Traitor and the Mob (14:43-52)

Violence now begins to come into the open as the well-armed mob returns, led by the traitor. The same trio we have dealt with from the start—the chief priests, the scribes, and the elders—sent them. These authorities preserve the fiction of their uninvolvement with violence by acting through surrogates. So we have an impressive presentation of the violence of this world in its several individual and institutional guises: a traitor, an armed mob, and religious, legal, and political functionaries, all behind a veil of surrogates. The act of treachery takes the form of a tender kiss, the intensity of it expressed by κατεφίλησεν (14:45).[25] Friendship and affection are suborned in service of institutional violence. There follows a burlesque of resistance when one of the bystanders—we

---

[25] V. Taylor, *St. Mark,* 559.

are not told that it is a disciple—draws his sword and cuts off a little piece of a servant's ear.[26] Then Jesus denies that he is a bandit (λῃστής) likely to put up a violent resistance, and as soon as the disciples have seen this, "They all forsook him and fled" (14:50).

Among those who fled was a youth who ran away naked, leaving his garment behind. We can think of no plausible way to integrate this incident into the logic of the text, excepting as an emphasis on the fact that all, absolutely everybody, forsook him and fled. Morton Smith thinks it is a historical reminiscence of the initiatory rite that Jesus required of those who wished to join his group.[27]

Jesus and Peter on Trial (14:53-72)

Jesus is led away to the high priest and [the priests, scribes, and elders] go with him. Peter follows at a distance and then sits with the servants, warming himself at their fire. The two figures of Jesus and Peter are thus presented as doubles but of a contrasting rather than a similar kind. The mimetic effect is reversed; the two become increasingly different, not similar, for the time being. The advent of doubles in a text is a trace of the GMSM because, in the course of mimetic rivalry, the rivals become more and more like each other until the distinctions between them are effaced. The appearance of the doubles is the sign of the sacrificial crisis. The special nature of the doubling of Jesus and Peter, and then of Jesus and Barabbas, as opposites rather than the same suggests that we are in the opposite situation from a sacrificial crisis; that is, we are in the sacrificial precinct where distinctions are clear and in the presence of the victim where differences are sharp, especially the difference between the victim and the mob.

The mob comes on the scene as the judges and witnesses against Jesus. They are all false, especially in accusing Jesus of threatening literal violence against the temple (14:56-59). We have already seen that the reference to the new temple is a metaphor of the resurrection, which the powers take literally as a threat to the ongoing life of the actual temple. The Gospel sees faith in Jesus as a better alternative to the temple but does not understand him to have threatened to destroy it himself. Nevertheless, by this accusation, Mark tells us that Jesus' enemies understand the threat he poses to their order.

---

[26] Ibid., 560.
[27] M. Smith, *Clement of Alexandria*, 167ff. See also M. Smith, "Clement of Alexandria and Secret Mark."

The juxtaposition of the messianic identity of Jesus with the destruction of the temple has no counterpart in Jewish belief. It has been argued that there was a tradition that the Messiah would destroy the temple but, as Dieter Lührmann points out, the evidence for that belief—in the Targums to Is 53:5 and Zech 6:12, in Lev R 9:6—is later than the Gospel.[28] Therefore, the interpretation of Jesus' dignity by relating it to the destruction of the temple is original with the Gospel, showing its understanding of him as the one who displaces the sacrificial system.

The trial before the Sanhedrin is the key to the passion narrative and one of the keys to the whole Gospel.[29] Here the innocence of the victim is revealed. The scene is carefully prepared in all that precedes (e.g., 3:6, 19; 10:33; 11:18, 27; 12:12; 14:3-9, 21, 25, 32-42), and there is reference back to it in what follows (15:10, 14). The reference in 15:10 to the envy (φθόνος) of the Sanhedrin underscores the unfairness of the trial and reveals the real, mimetic motivation of the priests. Jesus is the innocent victim of envy, and envy is the essence of mimetic violence; the verdict has been decided beforehand (14:55); the judges collude and no viable evidence is presented; the witnesses are suborned and contradict each other (14:56), and even the quotation that they attribute to him is inaccurate because, although he spoke of the destruction of the temple, he never said that he personally would be the one to destroy it.[30] This court has all the impartiality of a "people's tribunal" in a revolution.

Peter is outside while all this is taking place, a member of the cozy circle around the fire. Girard makes much of the fire and the accusation "You were with the Nazarene Jesus," made by the serving girl who recognizes Peter.[31] "Being with" is the sign of membership in a group—the group of the victim or of the victimizers. If Peter is with the victim, he has no right to share the fire of the mob. "Being with" functions by means of exclusion, and so the servant begins the process of expelling him from the gathering by identifying him with the criminal. She does this twice, imitating herself as it were, in order to unleash the mimetic momentum of the victimizer's group. The group then picks up the chase and introduces the cultural element—"For you are a Galilean"—as a basis for exclusion. Peter cannot return to solidarity with the mob; the mob will not allow it.

Now the figures of Jesus and Peter begin to converge; but as they do so at one level they begin to diverge at another. Whereas Jesus was silent

---

[28] Lührmann, "Christologie," 465.
[29] Ibid., 461.
[30] Ibid., 459.
[31] *The Scapegoat,* 152–57.

before his accusers and did not defend himself, Peter resists them with three fierce denials that correspond to the three warnings in the garden of Gethsemane. Three times Jesus had found them asleep; three times Peter fulfills the prophecy of 14:30-31 by denying Jesus. All takes place as in a nightmare; one of those around the fire turns on Peter, and his denial causes him to leave that circle of primordial human fellowship; in the courtyard the maid challenges him again, and he denies Jesus a second time; later, all the bystanders, the whole group, turn questioningly on him, ganging up to drive him out. Confronted by the group, he resorts to oaths and anathemas—which are signs of initiatory sacrifice[32]—in an attempt to join the mob, which is itself constituted by an unspoken conjuration, a group united in a conspiracy against the victim. All to no avail; and then the cock crows and Peter wakes from his mimetic trance. "And he fell down and wept" (14:72).

Jesus and Barabbas on Trial (15:1-15)

As Peter was the counterpart to Jesus in the action before the high priest, so Barabbas is the counterpart in the action before Pilate. They are not doubles but opposites, showing how distinctions are made by the sacrificial mechanism. Once again the authorities are named, in a slightly different order: the chief priests, the elders, the scribes, and the whole Sanhedrin. They bind Jesus, lead him away, and hand him over to Pilate. With the advent of Pilate, the roll call of the powers of this world is complete.

The juxtaposition of Jesus and Barabbas makes the point of the contrast between the two orders so vivid that it is almost a caricature. Barabbas is an insurrectionist and a murderer, a creature and a leader of the mob. We are reminded of the situation of the war that we saw clearly in chapter 13. We are told that Pilate sees the envy ($\varphi\theta\acute{o}\nu o\varsigma$) of the priests. Envy is the essence of mimetic desire and rivalry; it reveals the extrinsic nature of values with special clarity in that it is the urge not so much to have the object oneself as to deprive the other of it; the possession of the object is not the important thing, the rivalry with the other is.[33] The condemnation of Jesus arises only indirectly out of the Sanhedrin's envy. They do not desire something Jesus has; rather, their own inner-group rivalry can only be contained by the unanimous condemnation of the victim. Jesus

---

[32] Ibid., 156.
[33] Envy thinks that it will walk better if its neighbor breaks a leg.

attracts their envy to himself and so enables them to survive as a group. We have a clear statement of this phenomenon in Lk 23:12, "And Herod and Pilate became friends with each other on that day; for formerly they had been enemies." Jesus has done this all along as the roll of all the leaders shows. Leaders who otherwise would have been in competition with one another act in concert against him. The solidarity between the collaborationist Sanhedrin and the insurrectionist Barabbas trumpets the truth of the uniformity of violence across political divisions, and its shameless opportunism.

The priests incite the mob to choose Barabbas. Mark rubs our noses in the fact that we prefer the murderer to the man of peace, the sacrificial order to the spirit of God. Pilate tries to withstand the demands of the mob, knowing that Jesus is innocent. He cannot, because his power, like that of the priests, arises out of the mob and must respect its source. And so he sacrifices Jesus to the mob. The text is quite explicit on this; it reads, ὁ δὲ Πιλᾶτος βουλόμενος τῷ ὄχλῳ τὸ ἱκανὸν ποιῆσαι (15:15). The phrase ἱκανὸν ποιῆσαι reflects the Latinism, *satisfacere alicui*.[34] "To satisfy the mob" means to propitiate it by throwing it a victim. The very language of the text, therefore, shows that it understands the mechanism at work between Pilate and the mob.

Far from Pilate's being exonerated, as averred by those who claim that the Gospels whitewash the Romans and shift blame to the Jews, he is shown to be in exactly the same boat as the Jewish authorities, only somewhat weaker than they because he is unable to manipulate the crowd. His one attempt to do so, by offering to release a prisoner on the occasion of the Passover feast, fails because the Sanhedrin owns this particular crowd. Pilate is coerced by the mob, like every politician before or since, and has to give it the victim it demands. There is no attempt to exonerate Pilate, only a demonstration of the fact that those who control the mob control the source of power; Pilate's weakness reflects only this relative disadvantage: it is not his mob. If this were an attempt on the part of the text to ingratiate itself with the Roman state, it would be ludicrous; it shows political opportunism instead of the due process of law. To be sure, it condemns the Jewish authorities—not because they are Jews but because they are, like Pilate, the agents of violence. The text sees no essential difference between Pilate and the Jews. This fact alone should be enough to silence the claims that the Gospel is anti-Jewish.

---

[34] W. Bauer, *Lexicon*, ad loc.

Jesus Mocked, Crucified, and Killed (15:16–47)

The soldiers' treatment of Jesus shows the essential solidarity of the
Romans and the Jews in violence, for their mockery parallels the Sanhedrin's (14:65). The question that Pilate asks him, whether he is "king of
the Jews," seems to have been answered in the ironic affirmative by his
adversaries, for he is mocked as such by the soldiers and by those watching
him on the cross. The irony of the title for us, the readers, is that we know
him to be the king. A further irony is that the only one truly to reject the
mechanism of violence is ranked with two men of expressed violence,
crucified with two λησταί.

Jesus rejects the Davidic interpretation of the Messiah conclusively by
failing to come down from the cross in response to the challenge, "Let the
Messiah the King of Israel come down from the cross, so that we might
see and believe "(15:32). The chief priests and the bandits join in this
taunt; they demand the only kind of proof they can understand, an act of
violent self-affirmation; the priests want a miracle and the λησταί want
the King of Israel to leap down from the Roman cross and lead the armed
resistance. Jesus is not the Davidic Messiah of violence but the Son of God
(39)[35] and the suffering servant (Is 53:9, 12).

As if in response to the taunt, Jesus speaks the words of the sufferer in
Ps 22:1. The role of the Old Testament Scriptures in the composition of
the passion narrative is well known. Both Ps 22 and Is 53 tell of a righteous sufferer who is at present humiliated but in the future will be vindicated by God. The cry of dereliction is, therefore, not to be interpreted
psychologically but as an expression of the rejection of the way of violent
self-assertion in favor of a trust in God to vindicate him in the future.
This is of a part with the instruction in chapter 13 not to embrace the
apocalyptic hopes associated with the war, but to wait patiently for the
future vindication of Jesus as the Son of Man. It is the clearest statement of
the theme of the dialectical presence of God in the time of the Gospel.[36]

At the moment of his death, the veil of the holy of holies is torn and
the most sacred place exposed (15:38). There has been much discussion
of the significance of the rending of the veil.[37] The mention of it here

---

[35] Lührmann, "Christologie," 462–63, points out that the background of the title in
Mark is not the Davidic tradition of 2 Sam 7:14 or Ps 2:7, but rather the tradition that
goes back to the servant songs of 2 Isaiah and is mediated through sources like Wis Sol
2:12-20, and 5:1ff.

[36] J. D. Crossan ("A Form of Absence") spoils the dialectical balance in reading it as a
univocal assertion of the absence of God.

[37] See D. D. Sylva, "The Temple Curtain," where he lists representative scholars who
have argued respectively for its significance as a sign that Jesus' death has opened up a way

seems to interrupt the flow of the narrative from v. 37 to v. 39 and therefore it has been judged to be a later insertion. This is unlikely because it is an integral part of the overall argument. The suddenness of its appearance is intended to juxtapose Jesus and the temple as alternative places of divine presence. It is, in fact, the culmination of the verse that precedes it, interpreting the death of Jesus as the fate of the suffering servant at the hands of sacred violence. It is also the lens through which to read the centurion's confession in the following verse. The death of the servant opens the way to God for all the world by exposing sacred violence and depriving the temple of its mystique. These two vital interests of Mark's Gospel therefore receive a symbolic summary presentation in the rending of the temple veil.

It is not necessary in the light of all that Mark has told us of the displacement of the sacrificial system to search for any more recherché significance of the torn veil; neither is it necessary to ascertain whether the curtain is the one before the holy of holies or the penultimate one before the vestibule of the altar of the incense, the showbread, and the menorah.[38] The message, in any case, is clear: the holy of holies has been exposed to public view, its mystery has been removed; the system has been demystified and so deprived of the efficacy that depended on its operating behind a veil. Now we know what it sought to hide, that there is "no there there," only the figments of the double transference. The sacrifice of this innocent victim shows that sacrifice is just plain murder. When the veil of sacred violence is lifted, we see that there is nothing there, no blood-sucking idol, no devouring mouth that craves "the fruit of my body for the sin of my soul" (Micah 6:7b)! It was all a bad dream, and with the crowing of the cock we awake to the bitter truth of our own denial and complicity. Is it any wonder that we "fall down and weep" (14:72)?

"He Goes before You . . ." (15:42—16:8)

The pericopes on the resurrection and the great commandment give a hint of the nature of the new community (12:18-34). It is to be the work of God and it is to be characterized by love. Now the whole Gospel culminates with the resurrection; but it is not so much a presence as an

---

to God for humanity, a sign of the destruction of the temple, and a sign of the abrogation of the temple cultus. See also H. L. Chronis, "The Torn Veil." Chronis makes the unlikely suggestion that the temple is a symbol for the person of Jesus throughout Mark, so that the temple to be destroyed and rebuilt is his body, and the torn veil is the veil of his flesh that tears to reveal the face of God.

[38] D. Juel, *Messiah and Temple,* 140–42.

absence. The announcement is not, "Here he is!" but rather, "He is not here!"(16:6). What the resurrection symbolizes is not simply part of the present order, but something that belongs to the future. Here it is simply the power of the hope for a new order and a good future.

This is the context of our distinction between order and community. A new order can only come from the future eschatological reorganization of the kingdom of God. That hope, however, sounds in the words announcing the absence of the risen Christ. It is paradoxically kindled by the announcement of his absence because the absence is absence from the grave, a promise of the possibility of presence. "He is not here" is the good news of the possibility of future presence. In the meantime, the faith of those who receive the gospel is the foundation of a new community in the midst of the old order and the source of the energy of love flowing in the old channels cut by violence.

This kind of communication *per contra* is characteristic of Mark, and we shall return to the discussion of it. Here we observe the root of it in the understanding of the resurrection as an event whose evidentiary warrant is the imprint of its absence. Resurrection is not in the tomb, and it is not in the temple. It is in the faith of those who believe the announcement of absence and accept the invitation to follow Christ, who goes before to Galilee.

This message is directed specifically to Peter, that is, to us who have wakened from our mimetic enthrallment and need reassurance of forgiveness for our former denial. "He goes before you into Galilee" means that Jesus leads us away from Jerusalem, the place of sacrifice, to Galilee, the place of fellowship with himself. The "theological geography" of Mark, recognized ever since Ernst Lohmeyer,[39] is a major element in the poetics of the Gospel. The poetics of place conveys the message of the scapegoat, and the eschatological promise of a new nonsacrificial order is expressed in the phrase, "He goes before you. . . ."

It would be comforting if these were the last words of the Gospel, but they are not.[40] The actual last words are more somber and portentous: ἐφοβοῦντο γάρ, "for they were afraid" (16:8). Afraid of what? We can only conjecture. Afraid perhaps of leaving the shelter of the founding

---

[39] Kelber, *Kingdom*, bases his study on the opposition between Jerusalem and Galilee, and W. Marxsen, *Mark the Evangelist*, includes a study of "The Geographical Outline" (54–111). Cf. E. Lohmeyer, *Galiläa und Jerusalem*, and *Lord of the Temple*; E. S. Malbon, *Narrative Space*; W. D. Davies, *The Gospel and the Land*; and G. Stemberger, "Galilee—Land of Salvation?" in *The Gospel and the Land*, 409–38.

[40] Cf. A. T. Lincoln, "The Promise and the Failure."

mechanism, afraid of disorder and chaos. Can it be, then, that the Gospel ends on the note of the Grand Inquisitor? If so, it is not yet fully gospel, but only on the way from myth to gospel, somewhere in the time between fear and hope, bondage and freedom. The fact that it was later read as a sacrificial text to justify persecution shows that, to some extent, it is "in between." However, the later sacrificial reading shows more about those later readers than it does about the text; they were and are in thrall to the founding mechanism and so their hermeneutic was and is sacrificial.

Perhaps the best construction one might place on this final note of fear is to see it as an expression of realism at the prospect of life in the old order without sacred defenses, and the rueful realization that such a life is not yet possible. We are not able to live without violence even though we know it is satanic. Nevertheless, it is an advantage that our eyes have been opened and that we have once been awake, because now and forevermore, when we fall asleep again, our dream, like that of Yeats's Sphinx, will be "vexed to nightmare by a rocking cradle."[41]

---

[41] W. B. Yeats, "The Second Coming" (1920).

3

The Poetics of Place

The Way of Jesus as the Way of the Scapegoat (1:1—3:35)

There are traces of the revelation of the generative mimetic scapegoating mechanism (GMSM, see above, pp. 4–9) from the first words of the Gospel, but in order to highlight these traces we began with the passages in which they are most clearly evident—the passion narrative and its prelude in the events that take place in the temple. However, because the composition is (as I shall argue) poetically circular, it does not really matter where we begin. Indeed, as we turn now to the other parts of the narrative, to show how they make sense in the light of what we have established so far, we are also able for the first time to bring out the poetics of the whole Gospel. The pregnant silence on which the Gospel ends leaves us with two dominant images, one of the way (to Galilee) and the other of fearful disciples who fail to pass on the summons to follow the way.[1] These images are clues to the interpretation of the whole Gospel.

The Way Is a Spiral: "In My End Is My Beginning"

The driving out of the scapegoat is a movement from the temple to the wilderness (Lev 16:7-10). It is the way out of sacred violence. The

---

[1] Werner Kelber (*The Kingdom,* chap. 4) and James G. Williams (*Gospel Against Parable,* 97–104) recognize the importance of the "way" in the poetics of Mark.

"conflict stories" in 1:1—3:35 disclose the fact of the driving out, and the poetics of place present the process. The unifying spatial concept is, therefore, *movement in and out of sacred space,* and its dominant symbol is *the way.* We have already seen this poetics at work in the role of the temple as sacred center in chapters 11–16, and in the enigmatic note "He goes before you," on which the Gospel ends. The latter is a clue to the beginning (ἀρχή, 1:1) of the Gospel and to the basic theme of the way that gives coherence to all the poetics of place.

There is no consensus about the shape of the Gospel's spatial macro-pattern, despite the obvious differentiation between Judea and Galilee. The rejection of Jesus in his home town (6:1-6) and the repeated conflicts in the synagogues and towns of Galilee (1:14—3:35), make it impossible to regard Galilee as a place of salvation.[2] The conflict, hostility, and mis-understanding that come to a climax in Jerusalem build up throughout the narrative, both in Judea and in Galilee. The prediction of the passion in 10:32-34, which is usually taken to support the notion of the dark view of Jerusalem by contrast with the bright world of Galilee, should be read with equal emphasis on the verb "to go" and on the description of the destination. Read in this way, it expresses the movement back into the or-bit of the Sacred, not intimations of the hostility of Jerusalem in contrast with acceptance in Galilee. The real contrast is between the wilderness, which is the place of the scapegoat, and the temple, which is the place of the scapegoaters. Furthermore, the use of the verb προάγω and the pres-ence of fear in the passion prediction recall the ending of the Gospel (16:7-8), and suggest that the postresurrection way to Galilee is parallel to this preresurrection way to Jerusalem.[3] The emphasis in both cases is as much on the way as on the destination, and in both cases a theological destination has been substituted for the geographical one; in the former case it is the cross and in the latter, the resurrection.

The leadership of Jesus on the way is symbolized by his going ahead (προάγω, 16:7; 10:32), and this is foreshadowed by John's role: John goes before as the preparer of the way for Jesus, just as Jesus goes before us into Galilee (16:7). Right from the beginning, the Gospel establishes a mimetic relationship between John and Jesus that also links the end of the Gospel to its beginning in a way reminiscent of *Finnegan's Wake.*

The last sentence of the Gospel ends abruptly, and the first sentence be-gins abruptly. There is no closure to the last sentence and no overture to

---

[2] G. Stemberger, in W. D. Davies, *The Gospel and the Land,* 409–38.
[3] A. T. Lincoln, "The Promise and the Failure."

the first. The last sentence leaves the reader with a pregnant silence, the first sentence breaks into the reader's silence without warning, without a verb and without an article before ἀρχή, as if in telegraphic style.[4] The theme of both passages is: one who goes before to prepare the way. Could it be that Joyce was not the first to conceive of a work whose end is its beginning and whose beginning is its end?[5] If Mark is circular, then the journey away from Jerusalem following the risen Christ to Galilee will lead us back to Jerusalem through the adventures, conflicts, suffering, and triumphs that the gospel recounts.

Maurice Bloch describes the basic structure of a class of rituals that includes initiation, sacrifice, and cosmogony as a going out from natural vitality to the more enduring spiritual vitality and then a return to reclaim natural vitality in a new way conditioned by the experience of spirit.[6] He calls this pattern "rebounding violence." Violence drives out and violence returns to conquer. The going out from and the return to the narrative world of the Gospel recall this basic ritual pattern, which, I would argue, is not really basic but is a transformation of the scapegoat generated by the GMSM. Its existence, however, corroborates the role of the GMSM in the poetics of Mark.

The Gospel is in its circular composition symbolic of Christian existence, but because Christian existence is not a simple recapitulation of the life of Jesus—the resurrection lies between us and him—the Gospel cannot be another instance of the apocalyptic cliché that the end of time will be the same as the beginning (*Urzeit gleich wie Endzeit*). The end is different from the beginning because learning takes place along the way and because the end is transformation and not restoration. Once we have read of the cross and opened ourselves to the hope of the resurrection, the text is changed for us. The poetic of the Gospel, therefore, is not the circle but the spiral. Each time we follow Jesus into the Galilee of another reading, we have been changed by the power of the cross and the hope of resurrection mediated by the text we have just read.

The text is a circular composition but the experience of the reader is an upward spiral. Having read the Gospel once uncomprehendingly, we start again at the empty tomb and travel through the wilderness of Judea, the countryside and villages of Galilee and the Decapolis, several times across and alongside of the sea, fearfully back to Jerusalem, and to the cross, this time with eyes to see and ears to hear (4:12). This time we see

---

[4] This telegraphic style is part of an atmosphere of urgency generated by the frequent use of εὐθύς (1:12, 21, 29).

[5] Cf. D. O. Via, *Ethics,* 40–57.

[6] M. Bloch, *Prey into Hunter.*

and hear because it is Jesus who leads the way, not John. The journey can be free of the misunderstanding that plagued the original disciples, although not free of suffering and persecution. To us has been given to know the secret of the kingdom (4:12), but this knowing is a process, and those inside may possibly still be partially outside, in the sense of comprehending only in part. One can only begin to understand the spiral the second time around because understanding depends on witnessing the cross and hearing of the resurrection, and we must continue to read beyond the second and third times because understanding must continue to grow.

Even then, however, understanding can be inhibited by fear (16:8). Fear must have been a real presence to the persecuted community of the Gospel. Therefore, the disciples' incomprehension, which is so important a theme in the Gospel, is partially also a result of their fear. Fear is the opposite of faith (μὴ φοβοῦ, μόνον πίστευε, 5:36). Fear is the awe that gives the power of faith back to the GMSM (11:20-25) and makes Jesus a monster of the Sacred. The Gadarenes fear him because he healed the demoniac (5:15), the disciples fear him when he calms the storm (4:41), or walks on the sea (6:50), or talks of his suffering (9:32). Fear is the normal reaction to epiphanies of the Sacred, and it obscures the truth about Jesus. After the stilling of the storm, their fear leaves the disciples asking who he is (4:41), and after the walking on the sea, it leaves them with hardened hearts (6:52). They should have seen the power of Jesus over the sea as symbolic of the power of God over the primordial chaos in the Exodus crossing of the Red Sea, that is, as a sign of liberation from the Sacred. The walking on the water symbolizes the creating and redeeming work of God. Instead, the disciples see it as a proof of Jesus' status as a sacred hero, and they are afraid. They treat him as an epiphany of the *mysterium augustum, tremendum, et fascinans* rather than a symbol of the wilderness wandering far from sacred centers, and as a result their hearts are hardened.

Mark 10:32, the introduction to one of the passion predictions, is another good example (cf. 16:8) of the link between fear and the way. The disciples follow Jesus in amazement and dread on the way to Jerusalem, because they already intuit what he soon tells them, that he is to be crucified. Their awe-filled response is the response of mimetic rivalry, not the response of faith; therefore, they follow uncertainly and unfaithfully, ever ready to forsake him and flee (14:50). They do this because they see the way of the cross only as a path of defeat and not as the way of liberation from the realm of the Sacred and the way to expose the GMSM.

Because the women in 16:8 respond to their fear and not to their faith, no one follows Jesus on the way into Galilee. Therefore, he has to come again alone into Galilee and call for repentance (1:14-15). The spiral poetics of Mark is most evident at this point of the inauguration of the Galilean ministry. Just as Jesus goes into Galilee after his own arrest, so he comes into Galilee after John's arrest. Just as he singled out Peter as the special recipient of the invitation to follow him (16:7) because Peter had denied him three times, so Peter is the first one called in Galilee and the first to respond to the invitation (1:16-20). The term "gospel of God" (1:14) in a summary sense is clearly postresurrection, as is the claim that the time has been fulfilled. The promise of the imminent kingdom refers to the second coming, and the call to repentance has the misunderstanding and betrayal of the crucified one as its special referent. To "repent and believe the gospel" means to think not as humans do but as God does, and so see the cross as the revelation of sacred violence and believe the gospel rather than the Sacred. The pregnant silence on which the Gospel ends is to be filled, therefore, with the sound of the same narrative that has gone before, but this time the readers are truly to be those to whom the secret of the kingdom has been revealed (4:11).

This casts some light on the so-called messianic secret.[7] For readers on their second and subsequent times around the spiral, the perplexity of first-timers is ironic. Remembering the time when they misunderstood, they see that it had to be that way until they had witnessed the crucifixion and resurrection. Those who have not passed through these formative experiences cannot grasp the secret, therefore there is no point in telling them miracle stories. The miracle stories alone will not disclose who Jesus is but rather will mislead the hearers into taking him for a hero of the Sacred. This explanation is substantively the same as Wilhelm Wrede's, namely, that the secret is the result of a postresurrection reading of presurrection materials, but it is structurally different. The structure is not one of historical reminiscence being modified by faith commitment, but of a faith commitment using historical reminiscence to present faith as penetrating to the true identity of Jesus.

Creation and the Beginning
(ἀρχή) of the Way (1:1-13)

The introduction (1:1-13) serves to inaugurate and outline the image of the way, and to link it to its rich interpretive background in the tradition. Jesus is presented as perpetually underway, and the opening of the

---

[7] Cf. C. Tuckett, *The Messianic Secret.*

Gospel "foreshadows" this fact. It introduces the way as the beginning (ἀρχή) of the Gospel, by means of a double reference to the way of the Exodus in 1:2-3: "Behold I send my messenger before your face, who shall prepare your way" (Exod 23:20); "the voice of one crying in the wilderness, Prepare the way of the Lord, make straight his paths" (Is 40:3). ἀρχή in philosophic texts means first principle, but in a biblical context it recalls the first words of the creation narrative (Gen 1:1).[8] Here in the Gospel it signifies the beginning of history as the beginning of an Exodus journey with Jesus.

Creation and Exodus are poetically linked by means of the quotations from the Old Testament in Mk 1:2-3. Deutero-Isaiah, from which the second quote comes, understands the return from Babylon as a second Exodus and a renewal of creation.

Is 51:9-10 must be quoted here:

> Awake, awake, put on strength, O arm of the Lord; awake as on the day of creation [ὡς ἐν ἀρχῇ ἡμέρας, lit. "as in the beginning of a day"], the generations of long ago. Was it not thou that didst cut Rahab in pieces, that didst pierce the dragon? Was it not thou that didst dry up the sea, the waters of the great deep; *that didst make the depths of the sea a way for the redeemed to pass over?*

This passage is linked to the opening of the Gospel by the term ἀρχή[9] and to the passage actually quoted in 1:3 (Is 40:3) by the concept of the way. Behind it lies the Babylonian myth of creation through the violent division of the body of the chaos monster. It says that the making of the way through the sea was an act of the same power and significance as the creation of the world. History began when Israel left Egypt; and the way home from Babylon is the same as the way out of Egypt (Is 44:22, 28; 49:22; 55:12ff; cf. 41:18ff, 35).

The most accessible version of the myth, the Akkadian *Enūma eliš* ("When on high . . ."), provides a vivid account of the foundation of world order on sacrifice, and a dramatic vindication of Girard's theory. In the beginning, before there were gods, there were Apsu and Tiamat, the male and female presences respectively. They conceived and gave birth to the gods, who soon had to defend themselves against their parents. The gods killed Apsu first, which caused Tiamat to enter into

---

[8] Via, *Ethics*, 45; cf. Mark 10:6.
[9] Cf. Is 40:21; 41:4, 26-27; 42:9-10; 43:9, 12; 44:8; 45:21; 48:8, 16.

alliances with certain other gods to protect herself. She made Kingu her
new consort. Her enemies, however, found a champion in Marduk, who
killed Tiamat in single combat.

> Then the Lord paused to view her dead body,
> That he might divide the monster and do artful works.
> He split her like a shellfish into two parts:
> Half of her he set up and ceiled it as sky,
> Pulled down the bar and posted guards.
> He bade them to allow not her waters to escape.
>
> *Tablet V,* lines 135–40 (Pritchard, *Near Eastern Texts,* 67)

The cosmic and physical order was thus founded on the killing of the
monster. The human race, in turn, came out of the scapegoat killing of
one of the assembly of the gods, namely, Kingu. Marduk summons the
assembly of the gods and asks them who instigated Tiamat's attack on
him. They accuse Kingu:

> "It was Kingu who contrived the uprising,
> And made Tiamat rebel and joined battle."
> They bound him, holding him before Ea.
> They imposed on him his guilt and severed his blood
> [vessels]
> Out of his blood they fashioned mankind.
>
> *Tablet VI,* lines 29–34 (Pritchard, 68).

The human race, therefore, comes from the blood of the accused and
executed renegade god! Immediately after the execution, Marduk organizes the gods (Annunaki) into their respective orders above and below
and assigns them their tasks. They in return propose the building of a
temple as a place of their repose, and a throne for Marduk, which pleases
him greatly. The place of this temple and throne is to be Babylon and the
temple is to be called "The Sanctuary." (VI:35–59).

There could not be a clearer account of the generation of social order
out of the victim and the establishment of the temple as the center of this
order. The *Enūma eliš* is an exemplary account of a Girardian creation
myth, and it is alluded to at the beginning of the Gospel of Mark because
the Gospel wishes to give the lie to the notion that violence is the source
of creativity and that for us to live someone must be killed.

The Isaiah text takes a step toward demythification by interpreting the
myth of creation as a symbol of the historical events of deliverance from
Egypt in the Exodus and from Babylon in the return from exile. The

Gospel takes another step by interpreting the acts of historical deliverance as acts of faith in following the way of Jesus. Thus, the process runs from the myth of creation through the sacred history of Exodus and exile to faith, that is, in terms of the Gospel, from the mob, through the holy people, to the individual. The Bible uses the fable of the dissevered monster not to advocate or defend the order of sacred violence but to disclose and deconstruct it. The image of the monster in Is 51:9-10 is entirely poetic in the innocuous sense of aesthetic figuration. The crucifixion of the Son of Man shows the founding death of the monster and the necessary sacrifice of victims to be part of the mythic coverup of violence.

The biblical revolt against mythology, therefore, started before the New Testament, in the heart of the Mosaic faith. One has only to stand in the great hypostyle hall of the temple of Amon Ra at Karnak to be able with little imagination to appreciate the revulsion a Moses might have felt against the elaborate charade of the Sacred. As a prince of Egypt, he might have been present when the statuettes of Amon and his consort were bathed and given breakfast in a lavish ritualism that absorbed the wealth of millions and the energies of 120,000 priests. One could almost hear the sigh of relief when, once in the wilderness, Moses and his followers pledged allegiance to one formless divinity and swore never again to make graven images of the kind that cover the temple walls of Egypt. The massive sacral presence of Pharaonism is a compelling backdrop and foil for the Mosaic reformation and its austere turn away from the Sacred.

Moses and his band turned from the creation symbolized by the papyrus and lotus motifs on the great pillars of the hypostyle hall or the splitting of the chaos monster, to the path through the sea for the people on their way to liberty. The way through the sea—between the severed sides of Leviathan (cf. Gen 15:7-21)—and on through the wilderness, is the way out of the temple into the formless presence of Yahweh in the world. To be sure, the way through the sea is still not free of the Sacred, because it is presented in Exodus as a miracle that involves the massacre of the Egyptians, but as the prophet of 2 Isaiah interprets it, the image of Exodus refers to the simple historical event of the return from exile.

Thus, creation and liberation come together at the beginning of the Gospel as the baptizer prepares the way out of sacred space and into the wilderness. The new Exodus leaves temple-dominated Judea and Jerusalem and goes into the wilderness, to confess and be baptized (1:4-5). Baptism recalls the crossing of the Red Sea and the crossing of the Jordan by the tribes under Joshua (Josh 3:12—4:18), as if both the creation and the original conquest of the promised land were being ritually reenacted as a new start for the social order. The place where John was baptizing "in the wilderness" was probably between Jericho and the Dead Sea, which is also where Joshua crossed the Jordan when the river parted to make a path for the people. The associations with Joshua and the Exodus would, therefore, have been vivid in people's minds as they went out to John.

They would be leaving Judea and Jerusalem and returning symbolically to the wandering in the wilderness, and then by baptism crossing the Red Sea/Jordan into the promised land to start anew. On the level of creation symbolism, this passage from wilderness to cultivated land is also the passage from chaos to creation.

Beneath the narrative lies the awareness of the existing order as a structure of sacred violence centered on the temple that must be left behind if a new start is to be made. Therefore, all must experience the Exodus again. They must renounce their part in the existing order by returning to the wilderness. The community of the baptized is an antitype of the original group that was expelled from Egypt, wandered for forty years until their sin was atoned, and then crossed with Joshua. They constitute the true Israel.

The Exodus theme is deep in the New Testament. The Fourth Gospel understands the feeding in the wilderness as the antitype of the gift of the manna (John 6), and Paul understands the wandering in the wilderness as a type of the church in its temptations (1 Cor 10). The same poetics of Exodus operate in Mark and explain its spatial pattern in general as well as particular features, especially the centrality of the sea in the pericopes set in Galilee. To cross the sea and then feed the multitude in the wilderness is irresistibly Exodic in its symbolism (6:30-52), as John's Gospel makes stupefyingly clear.

Baptism as Taking the Way of the Servant (1:9-11)

The wilderness is the place of the scapegoat (Lev 16:10), and John the baptizer bears the identifying marks of the victim. We are told in detail what he wore and what he ate in order to point out these marks. He is the outsider and those who go out to him symbolically pass from the world of the executioners to the side of the victim. John and Jesus are, therefore, doubles. They both go before to prepare the way and they are both outsiders who bear the marks of the scapegoat. The obvious mimetic allusion in this doubling is intended in the course of the Gospel to counteract mimeticism by showing how doubles might coexist nonmimetically. John is quite willing to let Jesus take precedence, unlike the disciples, who argue among themselves who is the greatest (9:33-37; 10:35-45). Nevertheless, the relation between John and Jesus is subtler than the straightforward subordination of the former to the latter.

One purpose of the introduction to the Gospel is to present Jesus as the Messiah and to begin the transformation of the messianic idea away from sacred violence. The transformation begins when John fumbles the introduction. He announces that the coming Messiah is so much mightier than he that he is not worthy to untie the thong of his sandal; then the mightier one arrives and bows his head under John's unworthy hand. Matthew finds this so incongruous that he introduces a demurrer in the mouth of John (Matt 3:14), and some scholars argue by the principle of incongruity that a detail so unflattering to Jesus must be a historical reminiscence. Be that as it may, here it is part of a device for exposing the traditional idea of the mighty Messiah as false and replacing it with the humble Messiah of the cross.

The imagery of heaven splitting open and the Spirit descending like a dove symbolizes the transcendence of the source of Jesus' authority and his link with the chain of the rejected and persecuted prophets who were also bearers of the Spirit (cf. Matt 11:19/Lk 7:35; Matt 23:37/Lk 13:34-35; Gosp of the Hebrews[10]). The voice from heaven confirms the link with the chain of the rejected prophets (Is 42:1, "My servant [child] in whom my soul delights"), and adds the idea of the Messiah (Ps 2:7, "You are my son") and the Akedah (Gen 22:2, "Your son . . . whom you love"). Thus the Gospel draws the frame of reference within which Jesus is to be placed. He is the servant of Yahweh in 2 Isaiah whose work for God's justice entails rejection and suffering, and he is the son of Abraham, threatened with sacrifice for some mysterious claim against the lives of the firstborn. Both of these ideas are part of the conception of the messianic king whose coronation is praised in Ps 2, and all takes place within the frame of the Exodus.

The reference to the servant of God is a second indication that 2 Isaiah is prominent on the horizon of our text. At this point, it becomes clear that Mark has given us a clue to his interpretation of Jesus in the opening announcement, "as it is written in the prophet Isaiah" (1:2). The text of Isaiah is Mark's major pole of intertextual reference. We are therefore to

---

[10] "And it came to pass when the Lord was come up out of the water, the whole fount of the Holy Spirit descended upon him and said to him, 'My son in all the prophets I was waiting for thee, that thou shouldest come and I might rest in thee, for thou art my rest, thou art my first-begotten son that reignest forever'" (E. Hennecke, *New Testament Apocrypha 1:* 163–64).

look to Isaiah for the allusive depth of Mark, and we have already been alerted to the figure of the Isaianic servant of the Lord.

The quotations of Isaiah in Mark may be classified as follows: (1) They set the theme of the way of the servant at the beginning of the Gospel (1:3/ 40:3; 1:11/42:1); (2) they present the incomprehension of the disciples, the hostility of the Pharisees, and the ultimate rejection of Jesus (4:12/ 6:9-10; 7:6-7/ 29:13, LXX; 12:1/5:1-2); (3) they provide some of the graphic detail in the picture of the eschatological event (13:8/19:2; 13:24-25/13:10 and 34:4). The last apocalyptic ornaments might be discounted as end-of-world clichés, and so the substantive Isaianic quotations serve the theme of rejection. Jesus the servant of God is misunderstood, resisted, and rejected; nevertheless, he is the leader of the true Exodus and the bearer of the power of the new creation.

This newly designated servant son of God finds that the Spirit does not empower him to laud it over John but rather drives him out into the wilderness for forty days (1:12-13) to reenact the forty years of wandering and the forty days that Moses was on the mountain. The fact that the Spirit "drives him out immediately" recalls the driving out of the scapegoat.[11] Like Adam before the creation of Eve, wild animals are his only earthly company. The congeries of images and allusions, therefore, recalls the creation of humanity, the constitution of the people of Israel by Exodus and law-giving, and the scapegoat.

Thus, the first principle (ἀρχή) of the Gospel is the revelation of the victim at the foundation of the world, the archetypal human being driven by sacred violence to wild beasts in the wilderness. The message from heaven, identifying him as Son of God, transforms the Messiah from the agent of sacred violence into the suffering servant and the potential victim. The ἀρχή of the Gospel is the start of a journey that begins by going into the wilderness and continues by the way of the scapegoat, in and out of towns, synagogues, houses, and temple, and finally out to Golgotha, and on to Galilee, following him who goes before.[12]

---

[11] M. *Yoma* 6 describes how the goat was not driven alone but led into the wilderness by one designated for that role. In the Gospel, the Spirit performs this function.

[12] The theme of the journey is made more emphatic by Luke, who sets everything from 9:51 onward within the framework of the journey to Jerusalem. Luke also underlines the theme of leaving Jerusalem and the temple, when he alters the order of the temptations in Q to make the casting down from the wing of the temple the last of the three, with the effect that the ministry of Jesus begins as a leaving of the temple (Lk 4:1-12). Add to this John's (John 6) emphasis on the Exodus connotations of the feeding of the multitude and it becomes clear that Mark is working subtly with themes that were widely used in the earliest traditions.

Baptism as the Ransom
for Many

"Are you able to drink the cup that I drink and receive the baptism with which I am baptized?" (10:39)

The theme of baptism links 1:9-11 to 10:35-45, where the disciples misunderstand the nature of the messianic power and Jesus identifies his death as a baptism (10:38). The figure of the suffering servant, which we met at the Jordan, is also present here as the one who came "not to be served but to serve and to give his life as ransom for many" (10:45; cf. Is 53). These two baptismal stories bracket the first part of the Gospel. The major theme of the section is following the way of the servant/scapegoat, and the cost of such following. The first baptismal story introduced the exodus wandering of the servant/scapegoat; the second story concludes that theme[13] and prepares the way for his climactic revelation in the passion narrative.

We are told explicitly that the disciples do not know what they are asking when they ask to be seated on the right and left hands of Jesus in his kingdom (10:37-38). They misunderstand the messianic power as the violence of the sacred. Their request provokes the anger of the other disciples and Jesus has to instruct them all about the peculiar nature of his power—the power to serve and to give one's life (10:41-45).

How shall we interpret the reference to ransom in 10:45 (λύτρον ἀντὶ πολλῶν)? The literal pole of the metaphor of ransom is the buying back of hostages. In this particular application, a person rather than money is given in exchange for the hostages—Jesus goes into captivity instead of us. A sacrificial interpretation would have Jesus giving his life instead of ours to appease the wrath of a vengeful God, which does not fit the metaphor, because captivity does not entail the wrath of the captor and ransom is not the same as appeasement. A careful decoding of the metaphor has one person going into captivity instead of the many, and that makes good sense in terms of our theory.

According to our theory and in terms of the metaphor, Jesus went into captivity to the GMSM in order that we might be released from it. He gave his life as a ransom to the powers of mimetic rivalry, and because the mimetic rivalry is ours, strictly speaking he gave himself to us.

---

[13] The image of the cup ("Are you able to drink the cup that I drink. . . ?) is an indication of the link with the Exodus. The cup is eucharistic and, inasmuch as Mark presents the last supper as a Passover meal (14:12), it recalls the Exodus.

By dying, he unveiled the mechanism of our mimetic rivalry and thus enables us to turn away from it. He also gives us the Holy Spirit to help us in that turning. The traditional idea that Christ died as a substitute for us retains its validity, therefore, in terms of a nonsacrificial interpretation of the metaphor of ransom. He makes himself the victim of our violence instead of us.

That Jesus gave himself to the GMSM means that he was the only one who dared to live in this world of sacred violence without the protections of sacrifice. He refused to use "good" violence to drive out the bad, or even to protect himself. If all of us had lived like that he would not have died, but he was left alone at the critical moment, when instead of standing with him all turned against him. At that moment, the violence of our transgressions fell on him; our rage and cowardice broke against him. If we had joined him in a covenant not to inflict violence on the other and to bear the violence inflicted on us without retaliation, the wheel of sacrifice would have ceased to turn and he would not have had to give his life as ransom for many. The wrath that fell on him was human, not divine.

In terms of the traditional theories of the atonement, this explanation partakes of elements from both the "Christ as Victor" and the "moral influence" theories. The former sees Christ triumphing over the powers of sacred violence by his refusal to join them in their violence; the latter effects our salvation by showing us what these powers are, how they work, and how we might resist them by following the example of Jesus.

Jesus' question in response to the disciples' request, "What do you want me to do for you?" (τί θέλετέ με ποιήσω ὑμῖν, 10:36) foreshadows his response to the blind Bartimaeus in the next pericope (τί σοι θέλεις ποιήσω, 10:51). The two pericopes interpret each other and together provide the transition to the revelation of sacred violence in the temple and passion narratives.

Both pericopes are about the nature of the messianic power, as Bartimaeus's cry "Son of David" shows. The point of their juxtaposition is in the respective answers to the question of Jesus, "What do you want me to do for you?" Whereas the disciples ask for power at the right and left hand of the glorified Messiah, Bartimaeus asks only that he might see again. The disciples receive the teaching about servanthood, which they do not understand; Bartimaeus, who merely wants to see the world again, believes that Jesus can help him. He receives his sight and follows Jesus "on the way;" and that way leads to the temple and to the cross. The disciples are blind and the blind man sees.

Jesus' teaching on servanthood is an interpretation of baptism and Eucharist as a sharing in his death.[14] Only those who take the way of the cross can expect to enter the kingdom, but there is no determining of rank in the kingdom. The enigmatic "but it is for those for whom it has been prepared" (10:40) refutes the whole notion of prestige based on the order of this world, because the order in the kingdom is set by the impenetrable grace of God. Baptism as the rite of entry into the community is the rite of identification with the crucified, and Eucharist is the proclamation of his death until he comes (1 Cor 11:26).

Therefore, these two pericopes at the end of the section pick up the themes of the opening pericope, namely, the baptism of Jesus as a symbol of his death, which, in turn, is the summary symbol of his life on the way of the servant. This service is in essence the disclosure of sacred violence in the fabric of this world and in ourselves, especially in its religious manifestations. The first major division of the Gospel is defined by the idea of baptism as identification with the scapegoat in his rejection and death, which is, in turn, the beginning of the new creation and the way to freedom.

The Kingdom as the Community of Repentance (1:14-20)

Baptism is the rite of entry into the Christian community. The possibility of such a community, based on repentance, arises from the inbreaking of the kingdom of God and the revelation of the GMSM as the foundation of the present order. This is what the programmatic introduction in 1:14-15 proclaims, and what the paradigmatic account of entering into discipleship means (1:16-20).[15] Jesus announces that the kingdom is at hand and calls for repentance and belief in the gospel. Simon and Andrew, James and John, respond to the call and leave the structures of this world.

The advent of Jesus makes possible the transfer from one world to another, symbolized by the first disciples' leaving their normal lives to follow him, because it is the moment of the eschatological inbreaking of the divine ("The time—καιρός—is fulfilled," 1:15). The presence of Jesus and his revelatory activity is the presence of the kingdom of God. In this

---

[14] The cup is a symbol of the Eucharist and so we have a reference to the two basic rites of the Markan church.

[15] J. Marcus, "Entering the Kingly Power of God."

phrase, "kingdom" means power; Jesus is the inbreaking of the power of God to reveal, to heal, and to save. He reveals the GMSM and makes it possible to repent, that is, to leave the realm of sacred violence and pass over to the realm of the divine nonviolence.

The drama of what follows is structured as the contrast and conflict between two ways of being, symbolized by the contrast between the city and the wilderness, and between the wandering life of Jesus and the settled life of a Galilean fisherman and boat owner. In order to follow Jesus into the kingdom of God, one must, like Simon and Andrew, and the sons of Zebedee, detach oneself from the order of things as usual (cf. 10:28-31).

The relationship to authority in the new order takes the form of discipleship. The disciple lives with the master and learns by imitating him. There is no official hierarchy in the band of disciples, which explains why James and John could ask for the favored places in the kingdom. The master, to be sure, is set apart in a place of authority but it is an informal authority, and any hierarchy in the group seems to be informal, too.

The new realm, however, as we have seen (16:7-8), exists only in prospect; the gospel is not self-evident but has to be believed. This prevents the band of disciples from becoming just another sect of sacred violence within the old order of the sacrificial signifiers. In the meantime, we can repent, that is, detach ourselves inwardly from the present order of violence. Repentance and belief are closely linked. Faith is to leave the crowd and to follow Jesus. This can be done now while the old order still exists.

The Two Ways in Conflict: Jesus as Outsider (1:21-45)

Jesus and his newly constituted band of followers now are a metonymy of the kingdom, a part that stands for the whole. The community of the scapegoat no longer simply endures persecution but uses the experience of it to reveal and so undermine the authority of the scapegoaters.[16] The scapegoat community's real home is in the wilderness, outside of the normal commercial activities, and their authority comes from this transcendent place.

---

[16] I am reminded here of the remark of a protester in Prague, who after the November 17, 1989, beating of students by the police, said, "When one sees grown men beating fifteen-year-old boys and thirteen-year-old girls with clubs, then one knows that this regime has nothing left." The legitimacy of sacred violence depends on its being kept under wraps.

We are back with the question of authority (1:27; cf. 11:27—12:12). Formerly, Jesus was asked directly, "By what authority do you challenge the present order?" Here, the question is raised indirectly through the mouths of the wondering bystanders. If the mob is the ultimate source of authority in the present order, then these wondering bystanders as representatives of the mob question their own sources of legitimation by marveling at the new authority that eclipses the authority of the scribes.

The new teaching with authority is marked by its ability to drive out demons. Indeed, it is presented to us by means of an exorcism story (1:21-28), and so must be interpreted within an apocalyptic frame of reference that dramatizes the conflicts of the soul and society in terms of the imagery of demons and spiritual warfare. Indeed, the whole notion of the two orders, the demonic and the normal, should be classified as apocalyptic. Apocalyptic imagery must, however, be interpreted in terms of sacred violence, and in that case the demons are the mythological representations of mimetic rivalry deflected by the double transference onto a scapegoat.[17]

The demoniac in the synagogue at Capernaum is a scapegoat figure. He is unclean and outcast because of his affliction. The forces that make him outcast are the ones that recognize Jesus as their nemesis. The hearers of Jesus' teaching merely wonder about its new note of authority; the demoniac sees the threat that it poses to the order of mimetic rivalry. The fact that the demoniac appears in the midst of a teaching session in the synagogue shows that the demonic forces are at work within the normal channels and not, as the religious believe, outside them. Religion as usual is the place of the demonic, and Jesus is the enemy of both. The synagogue foreshadows the temple on the one hand and the circle of the embraced child on the other (9:33-37).

The demoniac is a scapegoat figure whose abnormality draws attention to him immediately (εὐθύς, 1:23) and who changes the point of focus of the whole scene. The mob turns in solidarity away from Jesus to the victim who stands alone at the center. The central location of the demoniac indicates that the synagogue needs him. Just like the Gerasene demoniac whom his fellow citizens needed so much they attempted to chain him down, so this demoniac is essential to the functioning of his religious community. The polity lives by its scapegoats.

The demoniac addresses Jesus and cries, "What do you and I have to do with each other, Jesus of Nazareth? Have you come to destroy us? I know who you are, the holy one of God" (1:24). He misidentifies Jesus as the

---

[17] R. Girard, *The Scapegoat*, 166.

center of the scapegoating establishment, calling him by the priestly title
"holy one of God"[18] and suggesting that he has nothing in common with
the outcasts, but belongs with the teaching establishment of the synagogue. Jesus silences the demon not because he wishes to keep the messianic secret but because the demon has deliberately misidentified him as
part of the sacrificial establishment, in a foreshadowing of the accusation
that he casts out demons in the power of Beelzebub (3:20-30). If Jesus had
accepted the title, he would have been unable to exorcise the demon because he would have been co-opted to the sacrificial order that generates
demons, and would have been part of the system in which violence is
driven out by violence. The pericope ends with the statement that Jesus'
fame went out from there through all the region of Galilee.

The fact of this fame is underlined by the following account of how the
house where he stayed was mobbed by those who needed healing and exorcism (1:29-34). The conclusion of that scene, "He would not allow the
demons to speak because they knew who he was," is to be read not as a
direct expression of the messianic secret but in the light of the previous
attempt by the demon to co-opt him. The demons try to counteract his
power by misrepresenting him as a bearer of priestly authority of the same
sacrificial kind as they represent.

But he belongs to those who have "gone out" or "come out" (ἐξῆλθεν,
1:35, 38). After the immersion in the midst of the old order, Jesus goes out
to the wilderness again. The normal interpretation of this passage emphasizes the reference to prayer as if Jesus were on a religious retreat, but the
emphasis is on the going out, and the prayer is incidental. The whole purpose of the "coming out" is the mission to the synagogues, which means
that the coming out is the basis of the message that he teaches in the synagogues. The phrase "for this reason I came out" (εἰς τοῦτο γὰρ ἐξῆλθον,
1:38) is enigmatic. "Came out from where?" one might ask. Luke (4:43)
answers "from God," which is more reasonable than the matter-of-fact
"from Capernaum." In Mark, however, the phrase describes the whole
event of his leaving the sacral structures, narrated as his going out to John
for baptism, out into the wilderness to be tempted, and coming again into
Galilee to preach the advent of the kingdom. The coming out is for the
purpose of preaching the gospel, and the link between the two activities is
so close that the one is equivalent to the other. To preach the gospel is
to come out of the sacral structures and vice versa. From now on, we are to

---

[18] Aaron is called ὁ ἅγιος κυρίου in LXX Ps 105:16; V. Taylor, *St Mark,* 174.

read every reference to leaving and entering as symbolizing the movement in and out of sacred space.

He then "comes into the synagogues" preaching and casting out demons (1:39), as if the scapegoat were returning to reveal the violence that maintains the order by driving him out. The demons are the markers by which the myths of violence identify the victims to be driven out. By coming out and going in, Jesus reveals the rhythm of exclusion. The pattern of entry and withdrawal with reference to the synagogue and the temple is a fundamental indication of the operation of the mechanisms (cf. 11:1-11).

The next pericope (1:40-45) of the cleansing of the leper introduces the crowd, which is the ultimate source of the power of the GMSM, in a story in which the institutional form of the sacral presence is still dominant. As a result of the healing, the crowds make it necessary for Jesus to remain outside. The dominant mode of sacral presence in the pericope is still institutional, however, as is clear from some odd and difficult words that suggest inner stress on the part of Jesus. He is "moved with compassion" (σπλαγχνισθείς, 1:41);[19] and he is "moved with indignation" (ἐμβριμησάμενος, 1:43). Furthermore, we are told that he quickly "throws the man out" (ἐξέβαλεν, 1:43), while telling him to go to the priests for certification. How are we to understand this strong note of tension, indignation, and barely controlled anger in the figure of Jesus?

It represents the reaction of Mark's Jesus to the ritual regulations concerning leprosy. The leper does not ask to be healed but to be cleansed (καθαρίσαι, 1:40), using the ritual terminology of clean and unclean. This infuriates Jesus but does not stop him from the act of compassion, which takes place suddenly as the result of the first waves of compassion/ indignation. This response arises out of the situation of sacred violence in which he is enmeshed because leprosy is so closely regulated ritually and so tightly tied to the sacred notions of clean and unclean.

This reluctant involvement with the cultus has the effect of driving Jesus farther out into the wilderness. The behavior of the cleansed leper arouses the inquisitiveness and acquisitiveness of the mob, and Jesus has to take refuge in the desert. It does not matter if one is execrated or celebrated, the attention of the mob and the sacrificial system make it impossible for the victim to exist within the system.

---

[19] Cf. the interesting textual variant ὀργισθείς in D and the Latin tradition, which suggests that anger could also be what moved him.

The Authority of the Son of Man on
Earth and the Nature of Faith (2:1-12)

Jesus "goes into" Capernaum again and into the house, presumably, of Simon and Andrew. The mob we met outside that house in the previous stay returns, and a question about authority comes up in connection with a healing miracle. The miracle is quickly eclipsed by the sayings that accompany it. Jesus forgives the patient's sins rather than merely healing his infirmity, and the scribes object to this usurpation of the divine authority. Jesus insists that his authority as Son of Man extends to the forgiveness of sins on earth. The eschatological judgment is present and faith in Jesus (2:5) is the criterion of acquittal. We might note again that the judgment is not inflicted by God, but is rather self-inflicted by means of the free response one makes to Jesus; no divine vengeance is implied in the notion of judgment. The authority of Jesus is the authority of the eschatological judge. His status as outsider symbolizes the divine transcendence.

The role of the mob highlights the element of faith. They make it impossible for the suppliants to approach Jesus in the normal way. Nevertheless, the suppliants are resourceful and find a way past (over) the mob, which Jesus remarks as their faith. *Faith is their determination not to let the mob get between them and Jesus!*

The reaction of the mob (ἐξίστασθαι, 2:12) foreshadows the situation in 3:21, where it is said to be "out of its mind" (ἐξέστη). The miracles of Jesus cause the kind of enthusiasm that has to be controlled either by the sacrificial solution or by some other means. In 3:30-35, we shall see how Jesus transforms the mob into a circle of disciples. In the meantime, we see the misgivings of the established powers about the threat to the sacrificial order posed by a human being who forgives sins and heals the lame. If the sacrificial monopoly on forgiveness is lost, then so is the institutional power of guilt, and if human beings ever discover that they can mediate guilt and forgiveness without reference to the established sacrificial channels, then the order of the GMSM is deprived of its psychological power.

Ritual Controversies (2:13—3:6)

The laws of ritual purity and their transformations are sacrificial channels for violence, and Mark now gives us a series of examples of Jesus setting those regulations aside in fulfillment of the claim that the authority of the Son of Man overrides the authority of the sacrificial system. Roughly at the center of the section are the metaphors of the new patch on an old garment and of the new wine in old wineskins. They pick up the point with which the previous section closes, "so that all were astonished and glorified God saying, 'We never saw anything like this!'" (2:12). Jesus brings the possibility of a new community, within but distinct from the violent order of sacrifice, and the transition from one to the other must be radical and not reformist. Even though it comes into being while the old order still exists, it is radically discontinuous with it.

The point of the pericope about the call of Levi is the saying, "The well have no need of a physician, but rather the sick. I came to call not the righteous but sinners" (2:17). On the face of it, this acknowledges that the scribes are righteous and have no need of Jesus, and that his mission is to support the religious establishment by calling sinners to repent and re-enter. This reading is, however, impossible in the context of the Gospel and so we must regard the saying as ironic. The well have no need of the physician means that the scribes mistakenly believe themselves to be well and so not to need to follow Jesus, while the sinners recognize their need and "many follow him" (2:15c).

Jesus strides along the *via maris* between Capernaum and the cosmopolitan border town of Bethsaida and enrolls one of Herod Antipas's customs officers in his entourage. This shows a cosmopolitan Jesus not afraid of the commerce along the great highway that led from Antioch to Alexandria, and at home in the company of the worldly men who lived along that road. The reaction of the scribes is the reaction of Jerusalemite xenophobia and parochialism for which that off-the-beaten-track hill town was notorious. The saying must, therefore, be read as an affirmation of the so-called "sinners" who are called and who respond, and a rejection of the so-called "righteous" who are overconcerned about the company they keep. The pericope is an attack on the exclusionism and narrow-mindedness expressed in the ritual laws governing the preparation and partaking of food.

The question about fasting (2:18-22) continues the revision of the practice concerning eating. It is not necessary to fast. The qualification in 2:21 that the time will come after the death of Jesus when they will again fast is the product of the tradition prompted by the resumption of fasting in later church practice.

Then follows a rejection of the law of the Sabbath in the form of a strong version of the already recognized rule that danger to human life warranted breaking of the Sabbath (2:23-28). Here mere human hunger warrants such freedom; what is more, in the face of human need, the category of the sacred dissolves, as is shown from Scripture by the story of

David and his men eating the showbread from the altar at Shiloh. The summation of the argument is that the Sabbath was made for man and not man for the Sabbath and this is shown by the fact that the Son of Man is lord of the Sabbath (2:27-8).

Thus, the freedom of the believer is again tied to the authority of Jesus as the Son of Man. The Son of Man warrants the nonritual forgiveness of sin and the freedom to respond to human need in disregard of the ritual regulations. *It appears that the Son of Man is emerging in this Gospel as a symbol of human resistance to the Sacred.*

The section of ritual controversies ends with another Sabbath confrontation, which brings the opposition to a head in a determination to destroy Jesus (3:1-6). It differs from the previous one only slightly in that the healing of a withered hand restores health while plucking grain to still hunger merely maintains health. Both cases emphasize the primacy of the human over the Sacred. Jesus is "angered and saddened by their hardness of heart" (3:5), a hardness that is precisely the attitude that serves the Sacred at all costs and sacrifices the human individual to the system.

The climax of the section introduces the prospect of Jesus' death. He has challenged and exposed the victimage system and now he is to become its victim too. We meet for the first time the two kinds of sacred authority that will contrive his death: the religious authority of the Pharisees and the state authority of the Herodians (3:6). From the Pharisees, he is stealing the religiously enthralled of the synagogues and, from the Herodians, the prisoners of avarice and expediency in their toll booths.

Representation and the Mob (3:7-19)

A great crowd from all over the area follows him. We are told where they are from to emphasize how big it is and how intense its interest. People have been drawn by the rumors of the miracles, which is an unworthy motive for seeking Jesus. Jesus separates himself from the crowd by ordering that a boat be prepared in case he should need it. The fact that he does not actually embark does not change the message of the boat, that Jesus is essentially separate from this crowd of miracle seekers. It also links this section of conflict stories with the following section of parables, which is introduced by having Jesus embark and teach from a boat. The boat symbolizes that Jesus is outside the crowd.

The symbolism of separation is rooted in the plot of the Pharisees and Herodians. They plot to kill Jesus and so we know that he is to be separated from his disciples by the cross. The symbolism of separation in the boat is continued and intensified as he goes up into a mountain and calls to himself only those whom he wants. A small group, therefore, comes out of the crowd in response to his invitation. They are to be the mediators and representatives of Jesus.

A new set of representations is being established outside of and parallel to the signifiers that operate within the crowd. The representatives are named one-by-one and constituted as mediators of the authority to preach and exorcise. The counterpoint between the small group of called-out disciples and the crowd is the counterpoint between the kingdom and the order of violence respectively. The crowd, on which Jesus has compassion (6:34) and from which he draws his disciples, is nevertheless the symbol of the lynch mob of the GMSM, and therefore the narrative has to show Jesus to be clearly separate from it, and the disciples have to come out from it in order to perform their function as disciples.

As long as the kingdom must exist in this world, it exists as a remnant within the overarching order of violence and is itself infiltrated by the treachery of the Sacred. One of the named disciples is to be the instrument of the GMSM in handing over Jesus as victim (3:19). The community of the kingdom is, therefore, not the kingdom as such but merely a representation of the kingdom, and a representation is always both the presence and the absence of the reality represented. The community of the kingdom both is and is not the kingdom that it represents, and this is shown by the presence of Judas Iscariot. Judas foreshadows the deformation of the church itself into a structure of sacred violence, and thus delivers the gospel from the charge that it is simply a piece of sectarian ideology. Like all truly faithful utterance, it undermines its own claims to absolute truth by revealing its own propensity for violence. Judas is a symbol of the church's own treachery; how sad then that he has traditionally been the catalyst for the scapegoating of the Jews!

Driving Out and Being Driven Out (3:20-35)

The forces of violence accuse the victim of their own crime and the themes of driving out demons and driving out the scapegoat come to a climax. The theme of driving out is most explicitly related to the fate of the demons whom Jesus drives out, and is therefore ambiguous because now the one driven out is the one driving out. Thus arises the obvious accusation that the analysis based on scapegoating is itself guilty of scapegoating. The text takes up the problem in terms of the accusation that Jesus is himself possessed by Beelzebub and drives out the lesser demons in the power of the prince of demons. Mark links this accusation with parabolic material and connects it with the account of Jesus' estrangement from his family.

In Girardian terms, the accusation that Jesus drives out demons by means of demons is a mythic version of the sacral procedure of driving out violence by means of violence.[20] The GMSM uses violence to control violence by transferring it violently to the victim. This does not succeed in getting rid of violence because Satan cannot expel himself and would never willingly allow his domain to be split. Only when he has been bound, as in the presence of the kingdom of God, can his realm be plundered. The exorcisms of Jesus are therefore genuine expulsions of violence by divine power and not just another turn of the screw inside the system. Those who interpret Jesus as an insider rather than an outsider and see his exorcisms as violence against violence, commit the unforgivable sin because they confine themselves within the cycle of violence and refuse the way out offered by the gospel.

The presence of the mob at the beginning of the pericope indicates the presence of the founding mechanism. The scene is again set by a going into a house. The mob follows him, virtually miming his movement (ἔρχεται . . . συνέρχεται, 3:20). Then we are told that those with him "went out to restrain the mob because it was out of control."[21] Thus, the mob, as the source of both the bad and good violence, signifies the presence of the mechanism. The raging of the mob brings to our attention the question of whether Jesus acts within the cycle of violence. The speculation and accusation of the Jerusalem scribes about the league with Beelzebub are perfectly understandable in the light of his popularity with the crowd. They accuse him of their own crime.

The exorcisms are not merely another turn of the screw of sacred violence, but a break-in to the system from another dimension and an opening up of the possibility of a new order. This new possibility has its application not just in the political but also in the personal sphere where it relativizes even the traditional ties of family affection and obligation. The

---

[20] Girard, *The Scapegoat*, 184–97.

[21] This is the most natural construal of the phrase ἐξῆλθον κρατῆσαι αὐτόν, ἔλεγον γὰρ ὅτι ἐξέστη, 3:21). αὐτόν must refer to ὄχλος in v. 20 in order to make sense of the statement, because those who go out are those who are with him, οἱ παρ᾽ αὐτοῦ. It does not make sense to say "Those who were with him went out to control him." The crowd, however, was so out of hand that it prevented him from eating (3:20). See R. Hamerton-Kelly, *God the Father*, 64–65.

mob is now transformed into the circle around Jesus (3:31-35) and recognized as those who do the will of God and thus as the new family of Jesus. The dramatic contrast between the mob in 3:21, which is "out of its mind" and has to be restrained by Jesus' attendants, and the crowd now sitting in a circle around him and listening to his teaching (3:32-34), makes the point that those who become disciples cease from being the mob that gives sacred violence its authority. The passage from rival to disciple is the passage from the lynch mob to the confraternity of the kingdom. Within this new context, the traditional family is an anachronism. The new radical fatherhood of God relativizes the claims of earthly parents and family obligations, which were in any case organized for the most part according to the forms of sacred violence.

The transformation of the raging mob into the circle of disciples contrasts with the rivalry of the Jerusalem scribes who accuse Jesus of their crime of using violence to control violence. They provide the foil against which the transformation appears more vivid. We are not told explicitly that the family members who tried to reclaim Jesus for the old order belonged with the scribes, but that is the implication. Therefore, we have in these pericopes an account in narrative form of the conflict between the Sacred and the gospel and the possibility of transformation of even the source of the old order, the mob. In terms of the parable in 3:27, this transformation is an instance of the binding and plundering of the strong man.

The poetics of place has played an important part in the communication of the message. We note the contrast between the temple, the synagogue, the house, and the town on the one hand, and the wilderness, the mountain, the sea (boat), and the open road on the other, between the urban and the rural symbolism of space. The movement from inside to outside takes place in terms of all of these places and shows that the important thing is the contrast itself (between inside and out) rather than the specific terms of the contrast. We note that Jesus describes his ministry as that for which he "came out" (εἰς τοῦτο γὰρ ἐξῆλθον, 1:38b). His progress into the center of the crowd goes through concentric circles of place, into the town, into the synagogue or house, into the circle of those inside the structure, and there at the center is a demoniac to be exorcised, a mother-in-law to be healed, or a tax collector to be called.

The symbol of the house is especially clear in the pericope about casting out Beelzebub by Beelzebub. It takes place in a house (3:20), and Jesus' response, which we are told is parabolic (3:23), focuses on the image of the house. "If a house is divided against itself that house cannot stand" (3:25) takes house in the sense of household, applying the image to rival groups. If the conspiracy of the surrogate victim mechanism is broken, the unity of the group will be lost. Unanimity is essential to the survival of the Sacred. The plundering of the strong man's house (3:27) is therefore the revelation of the truth that breaking the conspiracy disables the power of the Sacred. This is achieved not by inflicting violence but by suffering it on the cross and thus disclosing it. Jesus is the one who enters the strong man's house by moving from the wilderness into the town, the house, the synagogue, or the crowd, and there, by his death—by giving himself "a ransom for many"—revealing the conspiracy of violence that holds the group together.

4

The Poetics of Faith
The Group and the Individual (4:1—10:52)

Faith as the Dialectic of the
Group and the Individual (4:1—6:56)

The dialectic between the group and the individual defines faith and is the key to the central message of the Gospel. The crowd still does not understand the real nature of the kingdom, despite the fact that Jesus has made them a circle of listeners rather than a mob in search of miracles (3:34). Therefore we find him teaching from the boat, separated from them by the sea. This is the first clue to the message of this section—that Jesus and the crowd are distinct from each other. The disciples are in a privileged position with him in the boat (4:36). They allegedly have the ability to understand the mystery of the kingdom expressed in parable, because Jesus has instructed them privately (4:34), but, as we shall see, they are still prisoners of the crowd.

The Parables as Disclosures of the Divine
Power (4:1-41)

For Mark, the parables in this section are parables of prophetic disclosure, telling how the mystery[1] comes to word for those who have ears to hear

---

[1] "Mystery" is a technical term in apocalyptic literature for the plan of salvation, known only to select seers (LXX, Dan 2:18-19, 27-30, 47; cf. the use in the Wisdom literature, Wis 2:22; 6:22; 14:15, 23; Sir 3:18; 22:22; 27:16-17, 21).

85

(4:9), that is, how one learns faith. In Mark 4:21-25, which is the interpretive center of the section, the truth of the kingdom is compared, in the standard metaphor of disclosure, to a light that cannot be hidden, and we are warned to be careful how we interpret. If we get the interpretation right, we shall go on to greater knowledge and, if we get it wrong, to greater confusion (4:24-25).

Because of our primal attachment to the soil, the parable of the sower (4:1-9) probably does assure us, as Amos Wilder claims, that the world is gracious and that there will be enough and more for our needs, despite difficulties and losses. Like great art or music, this earthy assurance jolts us awake to the generative center of reality and nourishes our deep selves in what might appropriately be called an experience of the creative moment.[2] It is well named a "parable of advent" in the sense of the arrival of a gift and an assurance.[3]

In the Markan context, however, the parable emphasizes disclosure rather than advent. It tells us that, despite the loss of three quarters of the seed, the harvest will be as obvious as a lamp on a stand that is impossible to hide, either under a bushel or under a bed. The general principle to be derived from the parables is that "there is nothing hidden except to be made manifest, and nothing secret except to come to light" (4:22). They are parables of the disclosure of the kingdom as the spiritual substance of the new community, and counterparts of the disclosure of the order of sacred violence (GMSM) by the Gospel as a whole.

On this interpretation, the parable of the seed growing secretly is a parable not of the wondrous contrast between the seed and the plant but of the impossibility of keeping the seed covert. It is bound to show itself in the shoots that appear above ground. Likewise, the point of the parable of the mustard seed is not the contrast between the small seed and the large plant but that, although an infinitesimal thing can be overlooked, it will eventually be large and unmistakable.

The allegorical interpretation of the parable of the sower (4:13-20) applies it to the experience of the nascent church. The disclosure of the kingdom takes the form of the emergence of a new community. Over against the order of sacred violence represented by the temple stands the community of the victim. Nevertheless, three quarters of the new community misunderstand the gospel in one way or another. Just as the twelve disciples include one traitor, Judas, and one denier, Peter, and all "forsook

---

[2] A. Wilder, *Jesus' Parables and the War of Myths,* 89–100.
[3] J. D. Crossan, *In Parables,* 37–44.

him and fled," so the church includes those who do not accept the word properly or fully. Thus, the Gospel undermines its own propensity to become another myth of sacred violence in the service of another exclusive, sacred group. This new community is not perfect, but must live by repentance and faith.

The reason why three quarters of the hearers of the parable and readers of the Gospel do not understand and accept the word is that they are in thrall to the Sacred and its mythology, which can be decoded only in the light of the cross. The crucifixion has not yet occurred in the order of the narrative, and the readers who are reading the Gospel for the first time cannot at this stage understand the message of the kingdom. There are, however, some who are going around the spiral for the second and third time, and their grasp of the gospel is firmer. Thus, the community is divided into the members who understand and are fruitful and those who do not—those who are more advanced and those who are reading for the first time. This, I wish to argue, is the key to the interpretation of the fact that three quarters of the readers of this text and hearers of the word will not acknowledge the kingdom but rather will "see and not perceive, and hear but not understand" (4:12).

These unfruitful members are a counterpart to the frightened women at the tomb who, because they are afraid, keep the secret when the time of disclosure has come (16:8). The women demonstrate another reason for the unfruitfulness of church members, namely, their fear of proclaiming the resurrection and following Jesus on the way of the gospel. Those with such fear, even those who have read the whole Gospel and heard the full message, including the cross and resurrection, can be unfruitful Christians. The women at the tomb show that faithfulness is a matter not only of understanding but also of courageous action. Thus, there are two reasons why the gospel is misunderstood: (1) an ignorance of the cross and (2) a fear to proclaim the resurrection.

The Key to Understanding the Gospel

The parable of the sower is the key to all the parables (4:13). Whoever understands this understands the whole Gospel. We are at the point where Mark offers us the hermeneutical key. His theory of communication is contained in the parable of the sower, but not in the parable alone. The reference to Is 6:9-10 that intrudes between the parable and the declaration that it is the hermeneutical key (4:12) is an essential part of the key. It is even more important than the allegorical interpretation we have just considered, because it places the interpretation in the context of the intertextual relationship between the gospel and Isaiah, which has been operative from the beginning in the imagery of the way. The reference to Isaiah 6:9-10 is also particularly important because it shows how the violence of the Roman War influences the interpretation.

Isaiah 6:9-10 must be taken together with its immediate context in Isaiah, in accordance with Charles Dodd's principle that the quotation implies its context.[4] This can be convincingly shown in the present case in connection with the theme of the incomprehension of the hearers as well as the image of the seed. Here we shall take up the first topic, the incomprehension of the hearers.

The parable tells of how three quarters of the hearers of the word fail to appreciate it. The explanation designates them as outsiders by comparison with the disciples who have been enabled to understand. Soon thereafter, however, the disciples are asking who Jesus is (4:41),[5] and later they are said to have calloused or petrified hearts (ἡ καρδία πεπωρωμένη, 6:52; 8:17). In 8:17, they are asked, "Do you not know? Do you not understand? Have you a calloused heart?" In this respect, the disciples are the same as the Jewish opposition (3:5); these insiders are in no better position than the outsiders. Both insiders and outsiders are blinded by sacred violence. The theme of the hardened hearts of the disciples is central in Mark. Dan Via makes the *hapax legomenon* (σκληροκαρδία, 10:5) the key to the Gospel's theory of time. The claim that the disciples know the secret of the kingdom seems, therefore, mordantly ironic at this point.

Isaiah 6 helps us understand the structure of this irony and the theme of a hardened heart. Mark quotes the first two and the last lines of vv. 9-10 of Isaiah 6. What he omits are two chiastic triads of incomprehension: "Make the heart of this people fat (ἐπαχύνθη), and their ears heavy, and shut their eyes; lest they see with their eyes, and hear with their ears, and understand with their hearts" (Is 6:10). We assume that he took this chiasm about the (mis)understanding hearts as read because the theme of a calloused heart is prominent in what follows.

The theme is expressed by means of two terms in the Gospel, σκληρόω and πωρόω, and in Isaiah by παχύνω. The translation of παχύνω as "make fat" tends to obscure the community of meaning between it and πωρόω. Both verbs mean to thicken and so harden, in the sense of losing flexibility; σκληρόω is simply the general term for hardening. Therefore,

---

[4] C. H. Dodd, *According to the Scriptures.*

[5] This incomprehension is connected with their fear. Fear is the opposite of faith in Mark (5:6) and so the disciples fail to understand because their faith fails.

the theme of a thick heart is the result of the influence of the Isaiah text. Once again we see validation of the clue given right at the beginning, "Just as it has been written in Isaiah the prophet" (1:2), and are justified in looking there for help.

Isaiah 6 says that the prophet was sent by God to deliver a message to the people that would confound them until the cities were destroyed and the country laid waste. After that, the stump would begin to sprout again (Is 6:11-13). The most likely interpretation of this in the Markan historical context is one in line with Werner Kelber's notion that the historical context of the Gospel is the Roman War. Just as in Isaiah's time people could not understand the prophet before the cities were destroyed and the country laid waste, so in the time of the Gospel they could not understand the cross apart from the destruction of Jerusalem. The Gospel presents the point of view of an anti-Jerusalem faction of the church for whom the fall of Jerusalem and the destruction of the temple were essential parts of the revelatory event, but not the eschaton itself. The erection of the abomination in the temple revealed the violence of the Sacred in the midst of religion, and disclosed the real agency behind the crucifixion. In the hermeneutical context of sacred violence, therefore, there is more than a town and country issue at stake in the geographical rivalry between Galilee and Jerusalem. The fall of Jerusalem is part of the revelatory event because it is the ultimate rejection of the temple as the symbol and system of sacred violence and the founding mechanism. Nevertheless, most still do not understand its meaning.

The problem of why God should deliberately confound his hearers remains still to be solved. According to this criterion, revelation as a process of communication includes the deliberate encoding of the information to be transmitted. Via[6] finds in the Gospel as a whole three possible reasons for the failure of communication: (1) God conceals the revelation (4:11-12); (2) we willfully refuse it (6:52; 7:14-18); and (3) the social codes obscure it (6:1-6a). Reasons (2) and (3) are easily explained as the effects of sacred violence in its personal and institutional modes respectively. Hardness of heart, therefore, is the individual counterpart to the structures of sacred violence.

The first reason, however, that God conceals the revelation, requires more analysis. Mark 4:11-12, in which this claim is made, could be read "prophetically" as communicating an existing situation in a predictive way. Read literally, however, it says that encoding is part of the process

---

[6] D. O. Via, *Ethics*, 177.

of divine revelation, that God reveals in such a way as to make it possible for those who receive the communication not to receive the message. They may hear the words and see the deeds and not interpret them as significant. In such a case, there is clearly something devious about the mode of communication.

Our theory holds that sacred violence has corrupted our self-knowledge and our knowledge of God by means of the double transference, and that, therefore, we have to reverse the transference in order to get the message of the gospel. The divine communication has to be decoded, and this decoding depends on the disclosure of the victimage mechanism, which in the Gospel of Mark takes place through the cross and the facts that come to light along with it.

The first communicative relationship—between the signifier (victim) and the signified (the violence of the mob)—was reversed in the double transference. As a result, the victim of violence became its cause and the cause (the group) became the victim. The realm of the group is, therefore, the realm of a conspiracy to blame the victim and exonerate the group. This conspiracy must be unanimous to be effective. As soon as anyone speaks the truth, the conspiracy is threatened with dissolution, but the dissolution will not actually begin unless there are others who want to hear the truth.

In the realm of the conspiracy, things are backward: the victim is the murderer and the murderer, the victim. Therefore, communication of gospel must begin with a reversal of that reversal. For this reason, the divine revelation communicates *per contra,* through opposites, so that, for example, strength in this world is weakness and weakness, strength. The weakness of the cross is the power of reality; the strength of the order of sacred violence is empty and unreal.

Faith as Stepping out of the Crowd

Because this mythic world is maintained by a conspiracy of myth-interpretation, its stability depends on the unanimity of the crowd. As long as the mass mind buys into the conspiracy, the Sacred is safe, but as soon as an individual breaks ranks and speaks the truth, the conspiracy is threatened. *Mark calls this taking of responsibility for speaking the truth, this stepping out of the crowd, faith.* It takes the form of an active decoding of the divine communication that comes *per contra.* Faith sees the strength in divine weakness and the weakness in sacred power.

A message that requires an active decoding in the form of a faithful response is radically noncoercive. It is at the other extreme from modern advertising, which is the apex of communicative violence. It is also different from law. It never occurs in the apodictic or casuistic imperative but always in the indicative or subjunctive mood. Mark's theory of communication, therefore, moves in the direction of Jürgen Habermas's ideal of noncoercive communication, and lays bare its nature as the free response of faith to the individual other. Dominic Crossan and Robert Funk also lean in this direction with their theory of parable as a type of joke that causes fresh insight by the impact of sudden reversals of the normal direction of signifiers.[7] They tend perhaps to melodrama with excessively violent and apocalyptic claims that these reversals are equivalent to the ending of worlds; nevertheless they are essentially right. The divine revelation does not tear the covers away from mythology, but it does invite one to lift the veil for oneself.

Deconstruction Rather than Destruction

Such communication *per contra* is not the destruction of the sacrificial world of meaning but only its deconstruction, because all the counters remain the same while their semantic force has been reversed. The receiver of the communication has to decode it *per contra*. The literary term for this phenomenon is irony, and its interpretation entails the risk that one might misread it and so miss the disclosure of the kingdom under its opposite. There is also the risk that one's life will be changed if one reads it aright and hears the call to repentance implicit in such a reading.

The secret of the kingdom is symbolized by seed, to make the point that although it is hidden now it is bound to be visible and obvious later, like a stand of wheat in a field, or a great mustard bush. In the larger context, the secret is the revelation of sacred violence in the cross, summed up in the identification of Jesus as the suffering servant of God. The original context of Is 6:9-10 is the judgment of God that leaves the cities in ruins and the countryside waste, except for a stump, which the MT (not LXX) identifies as "the holy seed" (Is 6:13). In Is 53:2, the servant "comes up before him as a tender plant, and as a root out of dry ground." Thus, the

---

[7] I refer here to the "early" Crossan. Lately, he has lost his appreciation for humor and interprets the parables as social allegories. Jesus appears as a social reformer (*The Historical Jesus*). It is ironic that just as the inadequacy of Marxist materialism becomes clear on the political level it should resurge on the intellectual level in the work of an important scholar like Crossan.

Messiah and the servant are linked by means of the idea of the seed and the seedling.

The image of the seed, the blasted stump that bears the promise, and the unlovely plant that grows up unremarked, are the second important set of intertextual referents in the poetry of Mark 4. The secret, which three quarters of the hearers miss but which will eventually be unmistakable, is the divine dignity of the humble Jesus. This dignity is revealed in humility because, in the order of violence, truth appears *per contra* and not *per se*. Faith is the will and the gift to see through the scrim of sacred violence to the reality of the divine in the symbol of the seedling. To do that, one has to break with the crowd's way of seeing. In Mark, faith is to step out of the crowd and to see for oneself.

The Irony of the Excluded Insider

The fact that the disciples need special instruction (4:34) shows that they cannot spontaneously grasp the revelation in the parables. Their inability to understand becomes clearer in the subsequent miracle story which leaves them puzzling "Who then is this, because even the wind and the sea obey him?" (4:41). The miracle of the stilling of the storm introduces a series of portentous actions that disclose the mysterious power of Jesus and the essential incomprehension of even those closest to him. In the previous set of such miracle stories in the Gospel (the "conflict stories" in 2:1—3:6), the opposition is the religio-political vested interests; here, it is incomprehension and misunderstanding on the part of the disciples themselves. We are being shown how it is possible that three quarters of the hearers of the word could prove unfruitful, as well as the crucial fact that the insiders are in no better case than the outsiders.

This irony of the excluded insider is part of the poetics of sacred violence. Those who go into the house with Jesus for private instruction are no better off than those who remain outside because they do not yet understand the cross. They treat Jesus as the demons do, as "the holy one of God" (1:24), the messianic bearer of sacred prestige. The exorcism of the Gadarene demoniac (5:1-20) ironically underlines this incomprehension.[8] The Gadarenes, in asking Jesus to go away and leave them alone, not to tamper with the order of the Sacred in which they live, paradoxically understand Jesus better than the disciples do.

---

[8] R. Girard, *The Scapegoat*, 165–83.

The Gadarene Demoniac (5:1-20)

The demoniac is a classic scapegoat figure. He dwells among the tombs and wanders the mountainsides wounding himself and howling. No chains can bind and no man subdue him. He is possessed by a legion of demons, and legion is the mob of his persecutors. He carries his persecutors inside himself in the classic mode of the victim who internalizes his tormentors. He even mimes the lapidation by which he was driven out, compulsively belaboring himself with stones and crying his own rejection. He imitates his persecutors to the extent that he becomes his own executioner in the mode of self-estrangement characteristic of the mimetic crisis. The legion of demons is, therefore, the lynch mob.

The demons recognize Jesus as their nemesis and try to persuade him not to expel them from the system of violence altogether, but merely to transfer them from one location to another. To do this would be to manage violence by means of violence within the closed sacrificial system. Jesus, however, removes them altogether by sending them into the swine, which, contrary to the demons' expectation, rush into the lake and drown. The herd of two thousand swine is an eloquent symbol of the mob in pursuit of a victim. The herd's drowning means that violence ceases when the mob disappears. The order of expectation is reversed and instead of the victim going over the cliff the mob goes over!

We are reminded of the Tarpeian rock in Rome from which the condemned were pushed to their death, and that the Nazarenes, according to Luke (4:29), intended to hurl Jesus over a cliff, while Matthew (13:57) and Mark (6:3) say simply that they were "scandalized" by him. Execution by precipitation and scandal are traces of the GMSM. The water that the swine splash into is the standard symbol of undifferentiation, and the cliff over which they pour is the Tarpeian rock of precipitation. Thus, the demons, who are really the internalized crowd, fall victim to their own designs and tumble headlong into chaos.

When the swineherds report to the city and its environs, the populace comes out and begs Jesus to leave. The people do not want their scapegoats returned, and they do not want to see themselves as a swinish mob. They fear the revealer because he threatens the order of Gadarene complacency and deprives them of the comfort of the scapegoat. They do not want to break their conspiracy; rather, they want the scapegoat to remain in the shadows of the cemetery as a depository for their violence and a guarantee of their complacency. The fact that they had tried to chain him shows how much they needed him. They recognize the threat Jesus poses to the Sacred they inhabit, and they send him away.

Jesus acquiesces in their request that he go, but he does not leave without a trace. He sends the victim back, refusing his request to join the entourage. He sends him back to his home with instructions to tell his own people "how much the Lord has done for you and how he has had mercy on you" (5:19). The response of people to his message, however, is merely to "wonder," a response that does not indicate any real understanding. Nevertheless, from now on they have in their midst a constant reminder of an alternative to the order of violence in the restored and reintegrated victim whom Jesus rescued from the mob in himself and the mob in the city of Gadara.

The Woman with the Hemorrhage (5:21-43)

Having left the crowd before going to Gadara (4:36), and having met it there as legion, Jesus is greeted by it again as he returns to Galilee (5:21). As it presses against him, he feels the suppliant hand of the woman with a hemorrhage and is able to identify its special intention. She is the one person in the crowd who, in faith, is able to see the true power of Jesus—and she is a victim. She expresses that faith by reaching out from the crowd to Jesus.

In a community governed by a religious law that ruled a menstruating woman impure, she was perpetually unclean. She should not have been in the crowd at all because mere contact with her polluted. For this reason, she approaches Jesus furtively (5:27) and hopes to sneak away again unnoticed. Furthermore, she had suffered at the hands of physicians for the twelve years of her malady and has been financially ruined (5:26). She is a ritual and economic outcast. She is triply victimized, by the malady, by the community, and by the economy.

In all the jostling, Jesus registers the touch of the victim and calls her to the center of attention. She had hoped to slip away, and had he allowed her to do so he could have avoided acknowledgment of this illicit contact; instead, he deliberately calls it to attention. His public acceptance of an unclean connection recalls his touching of the leper in 1:41, and is part of the Gospel's rejection of ritual restraints on compassion. More importantly, however, calling the woman forth gives Jesus the opportunity to identify her act as the act of faith that saved her. "And he said to her, 'Daughter, your faith has saved you; Go in peace, and be healed of your affliction'" (5:43). The act of faith was to reach out from the crowd and touch Jesus, and then at his behest to stand forth and be identified.

It is remarkable that the emphasis is laid on her faith and not on Jesus' power. We are told that he felt power go from him when first she touched him (5:30); nevertheless, what the woman did is emphasized rather than what Jesus did. Stepping out of the crowd is the act of faith; it means leaving the conspiracy of the Sacred, going from the executioners to the victim. This movement alone is salvific without any need for mysterious power.[9] The need to step out of the conspiracy of violence can be seen intellectually and the step is healing in itself. Inside the conspiracy, the woman is constantly covered in blood; when she leaves it, the bleeding stops. Blood is the usual trace of the GMSM.

The raising of Jairus' daughter, within which the episode of the bleeding woman is set, develops the theme of the uncomprehending crowd in a negative direction. This crowd is the mourners who fill the house with lamentation and laugh at Jesus when he says that the maiden is not dead (5:39-40). The crowd laughs at the Lord in unbelief while the victims reach out to him in faith. The crowd must go if Jesus is to work a miracle (5:40).

The Unbelief of the Crowd (6:1-6a)

The theme of the unbelief of the crowd becomes even more negative in the account of the rejection of Jesus in his home town of Nazareth (6:1-6). The hometown crowd recognize his wisdom and miraculous power but are unable to believe it because of their preconceptions. They have him embedded in their mimetic network. They know his family and therefore it is impossible that he could be what he appears to be. Their ambivalence is well-described as "scandal" (6:3), because the dynamics of scandal are the dynamics of mimetic rivalry, of the model that both attracts and repels. Scandal begins with the assumption that we are potentially our model's equal and can always be the same as he. We want not only to equal but also to surpass the model; if we achieve that, he ceases to be a model. We do not want that, however, because the tension of our desire depends on his modeling, and so we desire a contradiction, to surpass and to be surpassed by our model. We attack and cherish, hate and love, diminish and exalt him. This is scandal, and it is the essence of anxiety (and addiction) because it is the love of what one hates and the hatred of what one loves. Mark tells us it is the state of the hometown crowd in Nazareth with respect to Jesus. The proverb that a prophet is honored

---

[9] In the reference to power going out of Jesus we have another instance of the mythic residue in the text, which we saw in connection with the prophecy of the crowing cock during Peter's denial.

everywhere except in his own home sums up the scandal. Envy is the power of the model/obstacle to attract and repel at the same time. The crowd wants to be like the other and to destroy him, because he is so pleasing.

The scandal of the hometown crowd makes it impossible for Jesus to work a miracle there. A miracle requires faith and he could find no faith in Nazareth. There is a progression in the treatment of faith—from the bleeding woman, who exemplifies it as the act of the single individual called out from the crowd, to the family of Jairus, which emerges from the crowd, to the crowd at Nazareth, which absorbs Jesus into itself and refuses to recognize any power outside itself. "And he marveled at their lack of faith" (6:6). Violence thus conceals the true distinction between God and the world by means of the false distinctions of the community of the double transference. The social role of Jesus makes it impossible that he could be anyone other than the son of their neighbors, despite the fact of his wisdom and power. This is the scandal of violence, which substitutes false distinctions for true.

Jesus Sends Out the Disciples (6:6b-13)

As the mass mind thus confuses the distinction between Jesus and itself, he sends out representatives to carry on his ministry (6:6-13). Just as he sent the Gadarene back to Gadara, so he sends the disciples out to do his work of teaching and healing. The fact that the Twelve are an already constituted group recollects 3:13-19, where he calls them from the crowd to be with him. Now he sends them away from himself as extensions of his ministry and presence. Behind this mission lies the memory of the ministry of the wandering charismatics, and its force is to emphasize the breaking of the ties of normal life. Like Jesus, who is rejected in Nazareth, his representatives are rejected and so have only a minimum of personal possessions and no fixed place of abode. As outsiders (6:12, ἐξελθόντες), they are able to call to repentance, exorcise, and heal, that is, counteract the depredations of the GMSM.

Herod Antipas confirms the inability of the old order as exemplified by the Nazarenes to contemplate something new (6:14-29). When he hears of Jesus, he assumes that it must be John the Baptist *redivivus*. He is at the stage of the mimetic disease where he sees only monstrous doubles. There may be a hint of this in the fact that the apostles go out in pairs. It is through them that Herod comes to hear of Jesus and immediately pairs him with the Baptist in the mimetic mode of complete identification. Herod's interlocutors are also locked into the myth of the eternal return of the same. They can only suggest that one of the prophets of old has re-turned. As long as Jesus can be located within the existing order as the recycling of someone already there, they need fear nothing new. This is a version of the hope that he is Beelzebub casting out himself. The circle of violence must remain unbroken.

The Death of John the Baptist (6:14-29)

The folkstory of the murder of John (6:14-29) provides another example of the power of the crowd, and amplifies the point that Herod is the prisoner of the Sacred. As king within that realm, he is the least free and the least powerful of the characters in the story. He is in a classically scandalous sit-uation with reference to John, whom he both hates and respects, wants to kill and protects. "When he heard him he was very much disturbed, and yet he heard him gladly" (καὶ ἀκούσας αὐτοῦ πολλὰ ἠπόρει, καὶ ἡδέως αὐτοῦ ἤκουεν, 6:20). Herod loved to be upset by John!

One could interpret Herod's situation psychologically. He lives in an Oedipal ménage, lusting for his stepdaughter and incestuously married to his brother's wife. His problem is not incest as such but incest with the wrong relative. John condemns Herod for the first incest, his desire for Herodias, and thereby gives energy to the second, his desire for Salome, provoking it by prohibition. Herodias hates John precisely for providing this incentive to transgression.

This kind of interpretation, however, does not take us as far as a mimetic one. We have three triangles: (1) Herod, Herodias, and Herod's brother (Herod of Chalcis); (2) Herod, Herodias, and Salome; and (3) Herod, John, and Salome. Interpreting from only one point of view within each triangle, we find these dynamics: triangle 1 is in the background as the explanation of why Herod found Herodias desirable in the first place; having bested his brother, however, he lost interest in Herodias because the obstacle constituting her desirability was re-moved; in triangle 2, Herodias as the incestuous wife is both the model and the obstacle for the incestuous relationship with the daughter. John's role is to provide the incentive for transgression with the daugh-ter by reinforcing the prohibition against incest with the wife.

He does this in a subtle way. Herodias is Herod's model/obstacle for the relationship with Salome. She models by being herself an incestuous lover, and she obstructs by being a demanding wife. John uses the model aspect to remove the obstruction; because the marriage is incestuous, he declares, Herodias cannot be a wife. Thus, in John's hands, the model pole removes the obstacle and opens the way to a new triangle with

Salome. This new triangle 3 comprises Herod, John, and Salome, a situation seen with dramatic insight centuries later by Oscar Wilde, and set to music by Richard Strauss.

We have no overt indication that Salome desired John, but John's moralism has the effect of his desiring her. John by implication prohibits Herod from having her, and prohibition is always the sign that the prohibited is desired by someone else. Thus, John provides a strong obstacle, and there cannot be an obstacle that is not also a model. Herod would read John's prohibition as saying that this girl is prohibited because God desires her, the ultimate source of prohibition being the envy of the gods. This obstacle would be the ultimate model and provocation, "to be as God!" That is why Herod loved to hear John preach the things that disturbed him greatly. Great prohibitions make great transgressions, and this kind of transgression, getting the better of a model one can never get the better of, is the essence of the erotic.

Herod is in thrall to his wife and stepdaughter and to John, but the clearest coercion comes from the crowd, represented by his guests. Having promised in the presence of this group of his peers to grant Salome's wish, he is powerless to escape. He cannot break the unanimity of the mob in pursuit of the victim, even though he profoundly regrets the loss of his obstacle (6:26). The loss to individual satisfaction is great, but the power of desire to bind one to the group is greater. Herod sacrifices private desire to group solidarity.

The pressure of the group is a fine instance of mimetic contagion, provoked by Salome's dance. The ritual of the dance recalls the sacrificial pole of the generative mechanism. Dance is one of the chief means for achieving the unanimity needed for the successful sacrifice. Here, it has been separated from its communal matrix and made into an opportunity for erotic display. Nevertheless, the undulating body of the young girl cathects all desire in the room, sweeping the group into a unanimous passion (6:22). She is the surrogate victim of the group's desire, which comes to word in the king's oath. He is compelled to substitute something for her because the mob now aroused will not be quieted without a sacrifice. So he sacrifices the thing unknown by promising in a solemn oath (ὤμοσεν πολλά, 6:23) anything up to half his kingdom.

Herod is at a fatal disadvantage now because he has shown his hand. He has in fact fallen into the trap set by Herodias who, knowing his desire for her daughter, had sent her out to display herself and thus infect the whole gathering with that desire. We learn that Salome is herself only a substitute for Herodias when the daughter has to ask her mother what it is she should desires (6:24). She is a representative of Herodias's desire to inflame the crowd so that it demands a victim, and then to give them John instead of Salome.

The party is transformed into a sacrificial mob by the erotic dance. The girl is the victim of the mob's aroused desire. Then Herodias springs the trap by substituting John for Salome in the desire of the mob, and Herod is carried along by his own desire, now deflected from one victim to another. The murder of John is thus a foreshadowing of the murder of Jesus at the hands of a mob.

Herodias targets John with sure instinct as the source of her husband's lust for her daughter, while inexperienced Salome thinks that John is merely an impediment to that passion. Both, therefore, have a reason for killing him, but only Herodias knows what she is doing. Girard makes much of Salome's innocence in asking her mother what she should desire as a sign of the fact that desire is learned. It is in any case clear that Herodias is the genius behind the action, but in the end the real killer is the mob, which magnifies Herod's passion by falling under its spell, sharing his lust for Salome, and thus fixing it as destiny.

Herod kills the victim under the coercion of unanimous desire in the mob, deftly deflected by Herodias from Salome onto John. As victim, John represents Jesus and foreshadows his death, just as the disciples on their mission represent his ministry. The section on the mission and the Baptist is therefore a presentation of the truth of Jesus through representatives. As the apostles return to tell of their experiences, Jesus himself reenters the narrative and takes them aside for rest and encouragement (6:30-32).

Jesus in the Wilderness; Exodus and Creation (6:31-56)

But there is to be no rest, because the mob follows along and is soon demanding not only attention but food. Jesus and the disciples are so busy that they do not have time to eat (6:31). When the crowd follows them even to their wilderness retreat, we expect indignation on the part of Jesus, but instead "he was moved with pity for them because they were as sheep without a shepherd, and he began to teach them many things" (6:34). This shows that there is also pity in Mark's dark vision of the mob. At the point where, in terms of the poetics of place, they have just expelled the scapegoat into the wilderness and even harried him in his place of retreat, the goat turns a pitying eye on his sheepish persecutors. They simply do not understand the source of sacred violence in themselves. In their victimization of others, they are the victims of their own self-deception through the double transference.

Then follow the miracles of the feeding of the five thousand and the walking on the water (6:35-52), which attest Jesus' power over nature but which the disciples did not understand (6:52) because their hearts were hardened. This information is an invitation to probe deeper into the meaning of these texts, and the deeper disclosure of these miracle stories is the Exodus/creation theme established in the introduction. The feeding in the wilderness recalls the manna, and the walking on the sea recalls the passage of Israel dryshod through Red Sea waters. The way of the scapegoat is the way of Exodus and new creation.

The section ends with the by now typical scene of the crowd thronging around Jesus to be healed and blessed, the pitiful multitude that was as sheep without a shepherd (6:53-56). We have been warned, however, that the hearts of the disciples are hardened. There is much more to come that they will not understand.

The Breaking Down of Ritual Distinctions (7:1-23)

According to our theory, ritual distinctions are made by the violence of the Sacred, and are particularly violent when they define the group by exclusion of the scapegoat individual or the scapegoat group. The following pericopes proclaim the removal of ritual distinctions among peoples and the possibility of an inclusive community.

In answer to the question of the Pharisees and scribes from Jerusalem, "Why do you and your disciples not observe the customs of the elders?" (7:5), Jesus accuses them of hypocrisy. The laws at stake are the obviously ritual ones, and the point is equally obvious: goodness is rooted in the inner disposition rather than in outer observance. The first case concerns the rituals of cleansing in connection with a meal. The rituals are examples of a hypocrisy that uses religious custom to avoid the real demands of God. The custom of Corban, by which one could free oneself of the obligations to support one's parents by dedicating one's resources to the temple, is a particularly egregious example of the antihuman tendency of the Sacred. The point is clear: one must not use ritual observance to escape from moral obligation; people must come before religion.

The "parable" that one is defiled not by what one takes in but by what one gives out is particularly elusive. In common sense and in ritual law, excrement, menstrual blood, and leprous suppurations are all substances that come out of a person and defile. In the explanation of the parable, however, we are told that excrement does not defile because it is the end product of what goes into a person and it is not what goes in that defiles but what comes out, and what comes out to defile is not bodily substance but moral action and attitude.

The larger point is clear—pure motives are more important that ritually pure action; but to make the metaphor work, one must restrict its negative reference to ritual having to do with food. The point is not a universal one, therefore; it is specifically directed at food taboos. Food goes into the belly and not the heart and therefore it cannot defile. Bad intentions come from the heart and they defile. The implication is that the Pharisees and scribes who challenge Jesus on these ritual matters are defiled by malice, while he and his disciples are undefiled because ritually impure food cannot defile. The passage is a specific rejection of the Sacred in the form of food ritual.

In what follows, however, the point is generalized to apply to all the boundary markers between Jews and Gentiles. We next find Jesus in a Gentile house in the Gentile territory of Tyre and Sidon (7:24-30). When a Syrophoenician woman begs for his help in exorcising her daughter, he refuses at first but then succumbs to her clever response and heals the child. The passage shows its linkage with what preceded it because the discourse takes place in terms of food—whether it is right to take the children's food and give it to the dogs, and, in response, that even the dogs can eat the crumbs that fall from the children's table (7:27-28). Jesus' refusal is based on the prior right of Jews, but it is so cleverly circumvented by the Gentile woman and so easily set aside by Jesus that we must conclude that it is a straw man. This is not an assertion of Jewish priority but rather its repudiation.

From Gentile Tyre, he goes to the predominantly Gentile Decapolis (7:31) where, through a particularly elaborate magical ritual, he heals a man who was deaf and dumb. Because this sort of thing was *de rigeur* for pagan healers, Jesus in the Decapolis does as expected of a wandering magician. We are again being told that external forms do not matter. It does not matter that he does not wash before meals like a good Jew and behaves like a pagan magician, just as it does not matter that he enters a pagan house in Tyre or extends the compassion of the God of Israel to a Gentile woman. Jesus is "all things to all people" and custom does not matter for him when it clashes with the opportunity to extend the power of the kingdom to others.

We may note that the healing takes place away from the crowd but in the presence of those who brought the deaf and dumb man to Jesus. So we have a limited circle of witnesses, like the household in Tyre, rather than the crowd as a whole. This is part of a theme of limited disclosure to the disciples and other chosen people who are commanded to keep the experiences to themselves. It does not amount to a "messianic secret," however, because, in some cases, like the Gadarene, the beneficiaries are actually commanded to spread the news. It is rather an indication of the negativity of the crowd's presence, inhibiting the free flow of faith and healing power.

The doublet of the feeding of the crowd (8:1-10), while reiterating Jesus' compassion for the mob (8:2; cf. 6:34), serves chiefly to introduce the controversy about the nature of the revelation in Jesus, and the problem of seeing but not seeing (8:1-26), that leads up to the confession of Caesarea Philippi. The disciples, who should be able to see and understand (4:10-12, 33-34), do not, but are rather in the same state as "those outside" (8:17-18). The Pharisees' request for a sign is disingenuous—they have already made up their minds to kill Jesus—but in the narrative it serves to show that the disciples are not much better because they witness the signs but do not understand them. The key, however, to understanding lies in the fact that we have a double telling of the feeding and its aftermath.

The differences between the accounts of the feedings are nugatory. The differences in the accounts of the aftermath are great but not so overwhelming as to erase all signs of relationship between the two. Both scenes are set in a boat on the sea and both involve the hardness of the disciples' heart. The walking on the water (6:45-52) is the sign that the Pharisees ask for in 8:11-13, and the feedings are the signs that the disciples do not understand.

Jesus warns the disciples against the leaven of the Pharisees and Herod and scolds them severely for their incomprehension, in terms that recall 4:12-13 (8:17-18). Then he pedantically compares one feeding with another, ending with the exasperated "Do you still not understand?" What is it that they do not understand? The mystical significance of the numbers *12* and *7*? And what is the leaven of the Pharisees and Herod?

The answer lies not in any detail of the two stories but in the fact that they are doubles, just as the Pharisees and Herod are doubles. Doubling is the sign of the sacrificial crisis. In the drama of sacred violence, the imitator becomes like the model. As this likeness increases, so does the rivalry, until the moment of identity, which is also the moment of violence, is reached. At this point, the antagonism has reached the level of crisis, the antagonists are doubles, and, unless the surrogate victim mechanism springs into action, violence will break out and order will disintegrate. The presence of doubles in the text is a sign of the sacrificial crisis and the loss of differentiation. The presence of double narratives in these sections of the text that prepare for the Messianic confession and the prediction of the passion in chapter 8 attest the generative presence of the GMSM. The leaven of the Pharisees and Herod, which the disciples do not understand, is, therefore, the Sacred.

Other examples of doubling reinforce this impression. The healing of the blind man (8:22-26) is a double of the healing of Bartimaeus (10:46-52), and in both contexts they occur just before disclosure of Jesus as victim. Furthermore, the blind man sees monsters, "men as trees walking" (8:24), which is another sign of the sacrificial crisis. Disorder is breaking out; things are doubling and monsters are appearing.[10] It is the time for the surrogate victim to appear and restore order by his death. This is what the disciples do not understand.

Misunderstanding the Messiah (8:27—9:30)

The confession at Caesarea Philippi (8:27—9:1) is a classic example of "knowing but not understanding" (8:17). Through Peter the disciples acknowledge that Jesus is the Christ, and through Peter they refuse his definition of the role in terms of suffering and rejection (8:31-32). They represent Satan, the closed circle of violence in which Beelzebub casts out Beelzebub. They cannot conceive of any other way of controlling violence than by violence itself; for them, the Messiah cannot be weak. They have entered the heart of the secret of the kingdom, yet at this moment of deepest intimacy they are farthest removed from the truth. The irony of the outside insider is at its most acute.

In response, Jesus summons both the disciples and the crowd and teaches the way of the cross (8:34—9:1). The disciples are no longer different from the crowd; they are equally uncomprehending, and equally inclined to be ashamed of the Son of Man and his nonviolent way in this violent generation. The redefinition of the concept of the Messiah that is going on before the eyes of the reader is opaque to the participants in the narrative. The crowd is innocently uncomprehending, the disciples mysteriously so. They are a foil to Jesus and the comprehending reader in a narrative marked by dramatic irony.

The promise that some present would see the kingdom come with power (9:1) is fulfilled proleptically in the transfiguration story (9:2-8).

---

[10] F. Neirynck, *Duality in Mark,* is a study of the pleonastic style of the Gospel. It would perhaps go too far to claim that duality at this level of detail was also generated by the Sacred. Nevertheless, this characteristic of the Markan style should be noted here.

The disciples are represented by Peter, James, and John, and the message they hear is the message Jesus heard at the moment of his baptism. It links his messianic identity with the servant of Is 42:1, and, by implication, with the whole of the portrait of the suffering servant (9:7). The glory of the Messiah, while unequivocal in heaven, is dialectical on earth, mediated through its opposite. The meanings of the titles "Christ," "Son of Man," and "Son of God" coalesce into the figure of the humble servant of God willing to undergo the suffering required for the success of his mission. The transfiguration story, however, like the miracle stories, keeps vivid before the reader the true dignity of this humiliated one.

Its Exodic allusions are also vivid. On a mountain like Sinai, attended by the two great figures associated with that holy mountain, Moses and Elijah, Jesus appears as the greater heir of the Law and the Prophets, and we are commanded from now on to accord him greater authority than Moses and Elijah. The old traditions are fulfilled and transformed; whatever sacred violence inheres in them is to be transfigured. Peter's proposal to build booths at the place of the revelation also recalls the Exodus through the association of booths with the feast of Tabernacles, which at one level of its significance celebrates the sojourning in the wilderness during the Exodus.

The transfiguration takes place while the rest of the disciples are enclosed by a crowd that demands a miraculous service they are unable to give. Thus, revelation takes place within a narrative context of unbelief (9:19). The pericope of the healing of the boy with the unclean spirit is especially revealing for our purposes and worth the following close scrutiny:

1. Jesus sees a large crowd around his disciples, and the scribes are arguing with them (9:14). The leaders, the crowd, and the disciples are beginning to coalesce into a lynch mob. Differences are being erased.

2. Upon seeing him, the crowd is excited and runs to greet him (9:15). It detaches itself from the leaders and the disciples and focuses on Jesus. The advent of Jesus reinstates differentiation, but the differentiation is curious. The question Jesus asks, "What are you discussing with them?" is addressed to the crowd, and the "them" refers to the disciples. The question, therefore, treats the disciples with a curious detachment, as if they were even more separate from Jesus than the crowd, and emphasizes the solitariness of Jesus. The disciples and the crowd are both distinct from Jesus now, as he takes on the loneliness of the crucified.

3. One person from the crowd answers Jesus' question and asks for help (9:17-18). The restored differentiation now reaches the level of the individual stepping out from the crowd, and the question of faith arises.

4. Jesus cries out in frustration over the faithlessness of this generation (9:19), in connection with the disciples' inability to heal the boy. The narrative places the issue of faith on the table as the central concern of the pericope.

5. Jesus takes the boy away from the crowd and, face-to-face with Jesus, the demon recognizes him and convulses the boy (9:20). The demon is like the crowd in this response to Jesus (ἐξεθαμβήθησαν, 9:15; cf. συνεσπάραξεν, 9:20), showing that the narrative recognizes the source of demon possession in the mimetic power of the crowd over the individual.

6. The nature of faith is explored further in the father's appeal to Jesus to help if he can. He is not sure that Jesus can help (9:21-22). This provokes Jesus' indignant response, "If you can! All things are possible to him who believes," and the father's, "I believe! Help my unbelief" (9:23-24). Jesus' reply indicates that faith is possible for everyone and that his own faith is not different in kind but only in degree from that common faith. The father realizes that his own faith is important in the transaction about to be made and utters perhaps the most human confession in all the Bible.

7. The crowd appears on the horizon, running to be a part of the action, and this causes Jesus to hurry the cure as if the presence of the crowd would interfere with the process. Indeed, when the crowd arrives, it misunderstands the state of the boy, thinking him dead (9:25-27).

8. Jesus explains to the disciples in private that they were unable to cast out the demon because they were deficient in prayer (9:28-29). This is clearly a traditional explanation from the point of view of an established congregation for whom the question of faith has been replaced by the question of piety. At the earlier stage of the tradition, the story is about the need for faith, not for prayer.

The poetics of place in this pericope tell us again of the generative operation of the scapegoat mechanism in terms of the crowd, the individual, and the Christ. When Jesus is absent, the crowd, the leaders, and the disciples merge into a single mob. His appearance causes differentiation to be reasserted until the individual emerges in the act of faith. Faithlessness refers to the state of the quarreling mob, which cannot help the stricken child. When the individual emerges from the mob to call on Jesus, his action is an act of faith, albeit imperfect because he is not sure that Jesus can help him. Jesus tells him that he must help himself by having faith, that is, by standing out from the crowd and taking responsibility for his son. Only away from the mob can the work of healing take place. Grace comes to those who act responsibly and do not try to hide in the crowd.

The redemptive role of the scapegoat is precisely to enable the individual to withdraw from the conspiracy of sacred violence by coming out to the scapegoat, by identifying with the one whom the crowd drives out. Faith, therefore, is intrinsically critical.

The Prophecies of the Passion

The prophecies of the passion (8:31; 9:12, 31; 10:33; cf. 14:21, 41) identify Jesus as the Son of Man, suggesting that there is a particular relationship between that title and the role of the suffering servant. There is no need to prove a precedent for this association in the Jewish sources in order to recognize that the Gospel makes this association. The formulaic prophecy first occurs immediately after the Petrine confession (8:31), and next follows the transfiguration (9:12). The third prediction (9:31) introduces the argument about who is the greatest, and the fourth introduces the request of James and John for precedence (10:33). It appears, therefore, that the first two present the somber reality of the cross to balance the claims of theological glory, while the second two present the humble crucified to balance the ambition of the envious disciples.

Thus, the prophecies represent a vision of the community of the non-violent kingdom in the midst of the order of sacred violence, and warn against being carried away by either theological or human ambition. The suffering Messiah is the embodiment of the new community.

The New Community as the Center of Salvation (9:33—10:52)

The third passion prediction (9:31) introduces a section on the nature of the new community. It is to be humble (9:33-37), tolerant (9:38-41), free of scandal (9:42-48), and exemplary (9:49-50). The hearers are the disciples only. This is private instruction away from the crowd (9:30, 33) although the incomprehension of the disciples is by now so far advanced that the privacy is compromised. It is as if the crowd had invaded the privacy and everything is heard in earshot of the final paroxysm of the mob. The disciples have been quarreling about who is the greatest (9:33-37), thereby showing that they have no idea of the nature of the new community.

The alternative to the conspiracy of the Sacred—to membership in the mob—is not the solitary, self-sustaining individual. To argue that would be, in René Girard's terms, to tell the Romantic lie of nonmediated desire. The alternative to the conjuration of the Sacred is a community in which desire is properly mediated by the divine, that is, a community in which acquisitive mimesis is replaced by the divine "agape" as the model of desire. In the Gospel of Mark, this new community is the community of the scapegoat, centered on the symbol of Jesus embracing the little child. These presentations of the ideal of the Christian community are in the nature of a definitive statement of Mark's vision of salvation.

The Inclusive Circle around the Victim (9:33-37)

The poetics of place are essential in the communicative strategy of this determinative pericope. They take us to the sacred center and show us there that the Sacred has been dethroned by the Servant. Jesus and the disciples are in Capernaum, in a house, and Jesus takes his place as teacher by sitting down. The disciples have been engaged in the old argument of envy about who is the greatest in their little universe (9:34). Jesus calls them into a circle around him (we infer the circle from the placing of the child "in the middle"), and teaches by word and deed. By word he says, "If anyone desires to be first he shall be the last of all and the servant of all" (9:35). Then he teaches by deed what it means to be the servant of all, first taking a child and placing it in their midst, and then taking it up in his arms, with the words, "Whoever receives one such little one in my name receives me, and whoever receives me receives not me but the one who sent me" (9:36-37). To receive rather than to expel is the mark of the new community of the kingdom.

The message in the symbol of the child is that preeminent dignity in the kingdom goes to the one who is "last of all and the servant of all" (9:35). Jesus' dramatic gesture of taking a child into his arms says that the greatest in the kingdom is the one who can receive those who have no power or prestige as if they were Jesus himself (9:37). This humility is clearly an antidote to the mimetic rivalry present in the disciples' argument about who among them is the greatest.

The poetics of place locate this act of inclusion at the center of space—in the town, in the house, in the circle, in the arms of Jesus. At the center, where in Sacred terms the holy absence skulks, sits Jesus with a child in his arms. The place at the center of the circle is the place of the victim during a stoning. Jesus and the child take that place. The gesture of taking the little one into his arms reverses the order of the Sacred. It dramatizes the inclusiveness of the new community by embracing rather than stoning or expelling the powerless one.

By means of this symbol and these poetics of space, the Gospel tells us that the new community replaces the conspiracy of the Sacred by neutralizing the power of envy. In the conspiracy of the sacred mob, envy binds the members to one another in the scandalous bonds of rivalry and desire. No one can afford to be found caring for the victim or siding with the weak, because that would be surrendering in the battle for prestige. The Gospel declares that such defeat is not loss but real preeminence in the order of the new community. The pericope of the child at the center is the summary symbol of the church as the nonsacrificial community.

"For Whoever Is Not against Us Is for Us" (9:40)

The Gospel safeguards its nonsacral nature by the device of confession, which it effects by portraying the new community as still infected with the Sacred even at this moment of greatest insight. The circle of the disciples, recently agitated by the struggle for prestige, is silent but not convinced by the example of the child. Soon they are excluding again. John the disciple puts this gesture of inclusion in question by objecting to the unlicensed exorcist (9:38-41). The Gospel narrates this here to show the frailty of the new community even at the moments of greatest insight, and thus to undermine its claims to perfection and so help prevent its own deformation into scapegoating violence. Like the receivers of the word in the parable of the sower (4:1-9), many do not or cannot receive the simple message of the child. Jesus' reply, "He who is not against us is for us" (9:40), expresses remarkable tolerance: All are to be included unless they take steps to exclude themselves. This is the "church" rather than the "sect" ethic, and it is a convincing rejection of sacred exclusionism.

How to Avoid Scandals

The extended warning against scandals (9:42-48) seems on the surface to be a stunningly sacrificial text. It commands one to cut off and throw away a hand, foot, or eye that causes one scandal, to expel the wrongdoer in

sacrificial style. Cutting (ἀποκόπτω, 9:43 *et passim*) is the essential sacrificial act, and the skill of the sacrificial butcher is most evident in dismem-
bering. Sacrifice is prescribed as the cure for scandal.

A metaphorical rather than a literal sacrifice is being prescribed. The
deconstruction of sacrifice has proceeded so far that the Gospel can use it
as an image to convey the moral injunction to resist envy decisively. Scandal, as we have seen, is to love the thing one hates and hate the thing one
loves. Scandal is envy, a desire to be like the other that is so intense that it
would destroy the other if it cannot be like him, and also if it can. The
injunctions to sever offending limbs are hyperboles expressing the urgency of the need to avoid the envy that comes from what one does
(hand), where one goes (foot), and what one sees (eye), envy exemplified
in the behavior of the disciples just narrated, in their wrangle about who
is the greatest, and their attempt to keep the privilege of being Jesus'
agents for themselves.

The sayings that close this section confirm the sacrificial metaphor.
"For everything will be salted with fire" (9:49) is an allusion to the customs of salting the cereal sacrifice and offering salt with every sacrifice
(Lev 2:13). The injunction, "Have salt in yourselves, and live in peace
with one another" (9:50), applies this metaphor in a moral exhortation
to behave so as to achieve the peace that the sacrifice achieved. We have,
therefore, a good example of how the language of sacrifice can remain
the same while its meaning has been transformed from the ritual to the
moral domain. The efficacy of this metaphor depends on the knowledge
that mimetic violence was traditionally controlled by sacrifice, a knowledge that Mark seems to have had either consciously or, more likely,
subliminally.

In the pericope of the child at the center of the circle of disciples, the
sacrificial structure of the poetics remains constant, in the sense that the
circle is the sacred center. The nature and direction of flow of the energy within the structure is, however, different. In the same way, the
structure of scandal is constant but the content and direction are different. One deconstructs scandal by recognizing its temptation and resists it
by resisting envy. Sacrifice has become a metaphor for moral action.
This expresses the insight that although there can be no alteration of the
mimetic structure of human relations in this world, there can nevertheless be a new mode of mediation, through the divine rather than through
the rival. Triangular desire can be delivered from scandal while remain-
ing triangular.

The pericope about divorce (10:1-12) begins by locating Jesus in
the same place where he was baptized by John and driven out into the

wilderness by the spirit. He is in Judea beyond the Jordan and he is tempted again (πειράζοντες, 10:2; cf. 1:13; 8:11; 12:15), this time by the Pharisees. The question concerns his attitude toward the Law of Moses. In response, he uses one part of the Law to set aside another, arguing that the account of creation (Gen 1:27; 2:24) takes precedence over the provision for divorce (Deut 24:1-4). This is a hermeneutical procedure of using the law to correct the law. The permission to divorce is not part of the fundamental intention of the law but an accommodation to the hardness of the human heart. The intention of the law is that marriage should be indissoluble.

It may be significant that the Gospel (10:12) envisages the unusual situation of a woman divorcing a man, thereby reflecting Roman, not Jewish custom. This strong emphasis on the high dignity of marriage could be construed as strengthening the position of women in the community, as could the next pericope on the welcoming of the children (10:13-16). This is a community that welcomes and protects the weak.

We shall not argue the merits of the prohibition of divorce here but shall simply identify the purpose of the Markan setting of the sayings: to show that Jesus has the right to dispose over the law. This point is made more vividly in the following account of the rich young man whose meticulous observance of the law is transcended by the summons to leave all and follow Jesus (10:17-31). In the instance of divorce, Jesus reinterprets the law. Here, with respect to the rich young man, Jesus sets it aside in favor of adherence to his own person. The question in the latter case is not one of observance but of intention. If the heart is hard, then no legal observance will justify it, and if desire is set on possessions, then no amount of observance will turn it to God.

In both pericopes, the action is followed by reflection with the disciples on the meaning of what has happened; in each instance, we hear the concerns of the Markan congregation in all their naïveté. In between the two pericopes is the account of the blessing of the children whom the disciples had tried to prevent from approaching (10:13-16). In all three cases, we hear the voices of those who have chosen to be outsiders in company with Jesus musing about their community as one that forbids divorce, welcomes everyone who wishes to join, and has given up the things of this world in the hope of a miraculous reward (10:28-31). They are outsiders with reference to the Mosaic law as well as to economic security and family relations.

It is appropriate that the section ends with the last of the passion predictions, spoken as they leave the place beyond the Jordan and ascend fearfully toward Jerusalem (10:32-34). Even as they ascend to the denouement, the quarrel about precedence in the kingdom breaks out again because they think that what awaits them in Jerusalem is a triumph (10:35-45). Once again, the disciples simply do not hear the prediction of the passion (4:11-12) and have to be taught that the one who is greatest among them must be the servant of all because the Son of Man himself did not come to be served but to serve and to give himself.

The new community of the serving Son of Man is, therefore, a non-hierarchical community in which the desire for God is more important than observance of the religious law, and in which women and children are cherished. Sacrifice has become a metaphor for humility and moral seriousness; it has become willing self-sacrifice.

5

Time and Space as Categories of Interpretation

Time and space are Immanuel Kant's two a priori intuitions of the transcendental aesthetic.[1] They are, roughly speaking, the categories in terms of which we organize experience. They cannot be separated in any experience of reality. For Kant, space defines the experience of things outside of the self and time defines the inner experience of things. Because they are categories in terms of which other things are experienced, time and space cannot themselves be the objects of experience. They are a priori intuitions.

We have used these categories in a literary rather than a philosophic sense. In a narrative, we experience the time and space of the plot in the event of the coalescence of horizons between the text and the reader. Therefore, a difference in the relative importance that one reader gives to one or the other of these transcendental categories must be adjudicated at the level of the interpretation of the text. There is no question of excluding one or the other category, but only of finding the right balance between them. We give space priority because the plot uses a poetics of place to reveal the mechanism of sacred violence, but that does not mean that we do not recognize the integral role of time as well.

There have recently been two interesting attempts to construe the Gospel in terms of time and space respectively. Dan Via[2] chooses time

---

[1] I. Kant, *Critique of Pure Reason*, 67–91.
[2] D. O. Via, *Ethics*.

and Elizabeth Malbon[3] space. Via brings to the hermeneutical moment the existentialist concern over temporality as the category of inwardness par excellence, and Malbon brings the apparatus of structuralism with its map of binary opposites. Like us, Via finds the hermeneutical center of the Gospel in the vicinity of chapter 10, but whereas he takes what the prohibition on divorce (10:1-12) reveals through the medium of time, we take what the child at the center (9:33-37) reveals through the medium of space. In the plot, both time and space mediate revelation but our preunderstanding favors space, and that predisposes us to favor Malbon over Via.[4]

Time and the Apocalypse

According to Via, the statement that the creator intended marriage to be permanent but had in the course of time to allow divorce because of the hardening of human hearts (10:5-9) indicates that the quality of time itself degenerated after the creation. The fact that now Jesus could command the permanence of marriage again indicates in turn that the quality of time has been redeemed and the possibilities of creation renewed. The quality of the time of creation is the opposite of the time of the hardened heart, and both times are present in the plot. The time of the hard heart is present and past; the time of the new creation is present and future. Time, as the symbol of the inner experience of the self with itself, has been renewed by the advent of Jesus, but the present is a period of mixed time. People still experience self-alienation (hard-heartedness) but at least there is now the possibility of creativity (perfect marriage).

This concern with time, Via and others claim, classifies the Gospel as an apocalypse. Apocalypses are characteristically concerned about the quality of time and about its beginning and end. They are, however, also concerned about the revelation of the divine secrets and the correlation between events on earth and events in heaven; that is, they present their message not only in temporal but also in spatial categories. We might take the apocalyptic symbol of the Son of Man as a test case of the relationship between time and space in the apocalypses and in the Gospel, and so test the classification of the Gospel as an apocalypse.

---

[3] E. S. Malbon, *Narrative Space.*

[4] Could it be that an unconscious modesty prevented Via from seeing the centrality of the image of the way, given that the Latin for "way" is *via?*

In the Gospel of Mark, the Son of Man is presented chiefly in terms of space rather than time. The relevant passages may be classified as follows: (1) The Son of Man coming in the future on the clouds or in the resurrection, that is, the traditionally apocalyptic image (8:30; 9:9; 13:26; 14:62); (2) the Son of Man as an authority and a servant on earth (2:10, 28; 10:45); and (3) the Son of Man betrayed, persecuted, and killed (8:38; 9:12; 9:31; 10:33; 14:21, 41). The spectrum of meaning runs from exaltation, through the authority of servanthood, to humiliation, with the emphasis in simple statistical terms on persecution, humiliation, and death (class 3 above). Two of the three classes use the category of space predominantly. The category of time is indispensable only for class 1, which contains the general apocalyptic image. Classes 2 and 3 are Mark's own contribution and should be given the most importance. Therefore, if one wishes, as seems reasonable, to maintain the link between the Gospel and the genre of the apocalypse, one must do justice to both categories space and time, and accept that apocalypse itself uses both categories to symbolize the transcendent. In the apocalypses, transcendence can be symbolized on both a horizontal (temporal) and a vertical (spatial) axis. On a horizontal axis, the mode is temporal; on a vertical axis, it is spatial. Something can be transcendent by being either "not yet" or "not here."

At this point, we must add to the apocalyptic model of the dual axes the narratological distinction between narrative world and plot.[5] The former refers to the totality of events assumed in connection with the plot, and the latter is the structure of the plot itself and its narrated events. Time is slightly more important in the former because the narrative world extends beyond the actual narration to the assumptions (past) and expectations (future) that it takes for granted in the readers. The narrative world exists in time because it is entirely an imaginative construction on the part of the reader, while the plot exists in space before the eyes of the reader in the text.

The proper relationship between time and space is, therefore, among other things, a function of the relationship between narrative world and plot, and between the inner experience of self-relatedness and the outer experience of other-relatedness. To the extent that communication is an inner event, it happens in time because it is the coalescence of horizons and a horizon lies along the horizontal (temporal) axis of assumption and expectation ("already and not yet"). To the extent that communication

---

[5] Via, *Ethics,* 31.

is a relational event, it happens in space because the self and the other are separated along the vertical (spatial) axis of "here and there."

In these apocalyptic terms, time and space are one at the point of intersection of the vertical and horizontal axes. That point is temporally the present and spatially the center, and meaning *presents* itself by *taking place* there. As such an event, meaning is always an act of violence because the center is the Sacred, the place of the victim. The victim is the primal signifier, the one made sacred by being violently separated from the group, so that he can reflect ourselves to ourselves. Because all the signifiers have been put in place by this violence and myth-interpreted by the double transference, meaning is violent. It coerces us, subdues our fantasy, and fixes our freedom to the rack of "reality"; but this "reality" is ever only its own mythic version. Meaning "presents" itself violently by "taking place," and that is why the presence of the Son of Man on earth takes place as the suffering servant whose way is the *eccentric* way of the scapegoat and whose death reveals the mythic nothingness of the center (15:37-39). To demythify the world, we must move with the scapegoat, away from the center to the new noncoercive meaning of gospel, in whose realm the signifiers are not secured by sacred violence.

In the order of sacred violence, the present is primary; the past and the future depend on it because they are the memory and expectation respectively of the person at the center. The authority of kings and heroes defines the parameters of hope and memory for the masses. In gospel, the future is primary, and the present is a disappearing moment through which anticipation passes on its way to memory. There is no hero at the center to impose meaning on us. The "hero" of the Gospel is crucified and thus removed as a sacred presence. In these terms, the primary category of the Sacred is space, and that of the gospel is time, and the interaction of the two in Mark is the interaction of gospel and the Sacred. However, because gospel is a critique of the Sacred, the poetics of place counters the Sacred in its own terms, and thus, in the plot, privileges the category of space. In the narrative world, however, it privileges time, because the movement away from the sacred center is a movement from the present to the future, from the Sacred in the temple to the hope for the advent of the Son of Man.

Time and space, therefore, belong together as transcendental categories of interpretation in Mark, and their interaction is best understood through a consideration of the image of "the way." In Mark, the narrative circularity of the plot adds a note of subtlety, but the concept of the way mediates rather than complicates the difference between the two categories. Malbon[6] spotted the fact that, on the structuralist calculus, the way mediates the difference between chaos and order. On the level of narratology, however, it mediates the difference between time and space. To "go before" is to "go ahead" and to "go earlier." Mark holds both these meanings together by the image of the way, with a slight preference for the former within the narrative plot and a slight preference for the latter within the narrative world.

In the phrase, "He has gone before you (προάγω)" (16:7), "before" could have the double meaning of "ahead of you" and "earlier than you." He has gone ahead of us, leading the way out of Jerusalem to Galilee where we shall see him again, and he has gone earlier than we as the pioneer of the new way. The spatial sense predominates in the plot because the image of following Jesus on the way is already dominant in the Gospel's understanding of discipleship and there are many foreshadowings of this final declaration (6:45; 10:32; 14:28). In the plot, the promise of renewed fellowship with the absent Lord will happen a-way from Jerusalem, in Galilee.

The way, however, is also an ethical metaphor for Christian existence in the time after the resurrection of Jesus, that is, in the narrative world. Jesus is no longer literally present and so does not take place, excepting as re-presented through the memory of the believer. Re-presentation is a mode in which time displaces space because the risen Jesus takes place through the temporal modality of memory. In terms of the axis of time and space, the movement from presentation to re-presentation is a move away from the center along the horizontal (temporal) axis, and thus a crossing of the apocalyptic lines of distinction between the two categories. It is "not being there" by "not being present" (16:6). Within the horizon of sacred violence, it is a temporal move away from the sacred center, and the temporal shift from presence to re-presentation is equivalent to the spatial shift from the center to the margin, from the metaphysics of presence to the metaphysics of faith.

In the narrative world of Mark, the relationship between space and time is mediated by the way of the reader through the circularity of the composition. Beyond the first reading lies the second and the third, as one continues to read with increasing comprehension and to live with increasing fidelity the vision of the narrative. Time, therefore, continues in the form of the circular reading of the text, and thus time and space

---

are blended in the traditional Aristotelian image of time as movement in a circle.

Via's understanding of time is too romantic. He makes too much of a sentiment of Gérard Genette, which he presents as follows: "The first time—the first kiss, first sight of the sea, first evening at a particular hotel, first dinner with certain friends—'to the very extent to which one experiences its inaugural value intensely, is at the same time always (already) a last time—if only because it is forever the last to have been first, and after it, inevitably, the sway of repetition and habit begins.'"[7] To this he adds Nicholas Berdyaev's lament over the "congealing or coagulation of freedom" in the course of history.

This is existentialist romanticism in spades: only the first time is fully significant and repetition is inevitably sclerotic! The first time, however, is often catastrophically unsatisfying and experience adds greatly to the significance and enjoyment. "The first kiss," which Via puts in first place among his examples, is often embarrassingly callow to the retrospect of the mature lover. To expect that thrill of the beginning to persist throughout a marriage is a recipe for divorce, and so on psychological grounds alone this form of the idea of the mutual entailment of beginning and end is less than satisfactory. On the evidence of the Gospel, there is no warrant for the celebration of the first time. The image of creation in the Gospel signifies creativity rather than primitivity. Freshness is not a function of firstness but of authority in the sense of authenticity (from αὐξάνω, to grow, increase, become strong). Creativity was remarked by those who recognized the note of renewed authority in the voice of Jesus (1:27).

Via wants to describe the apocalyptic overlap of the ages in Mark that Joachim Jeremias once described as "inaugurated eschatology." This is still an adequate description of the phenomenon of the interweaving of the old and the new world, the hardening and the healing powers at work in the Gospel. If the ethical efficacy of the Gospel depends on the congruence between its experience of revelation through time and the reader's experience of the same, then it is sufficient to remark that we, like the Gospel of Mark, experience the time of our lives as a mixed bag of hardness and healing. The spin that the Gospel puts on this common experience is to claim that the good times will ultimately prevail and that therefore we can look forward to a good future. In the apocalyptic language of the Gospel, the time is fulfilled, the kingdom of God is near, appears from time to time, and will be vindicated in the future. But all

---

[7] Via, *Ethics,* 29.

this has to be a matter of faith because Jesus was driven out and has gone before us.

Thus we are led back to the dominant image of the way. The reader is to follow the way of Jesus and conduct his or her life according to Jesus' example. In terms of the whole Gospel, this example is one of nonresistance to violence and noncooperation with its institutions. It is to accept the scapegoats rather than to drive them out, and to resist the deception of religion. This is spelled out predominantly by the poetics of space rather than of time.

Space and the Architecture of Order

If Via errs in overemphasizing the category of time, Malbon errs in the same way with space. Her structuralist account of space in Mark, which confirms the essential points of our interpretation despite its different approach, classifies three general types of space in the plot: (1) geopolitical—Judea, Galilee, and foreign lands; (2) topographical—way, wilderness, mountain, sea, and inhabited areas; (3) architectural—temple, synagogue, and house. Generally speaking, geopolitical space provides the overarching order, topographical space dominates chapters 1–10, and architectural, chapters 11–16. This latter classification is very rough; there is a lot of architectural space in chapters 1–9, as we have noted with reference to the role of the synagogue and house settings in those chapters. Malbon's topographical analysis confirms our use of the Exodus as an interpretive context. Its significant items—way, sea, wilderness,[8] and mountain—are essential Exodic motifs. The architectural categories have been crucial for our analysis of the poetics of space. The temple/synagogue/house is the inside and center that is primordially the place of sacrifice.

We have already expounded the significance of the topographical phenomenology. Here we shall make explicit the significance of the architectural images. The first demarcation between chaos and order took the form of spatial separation between the area inside the walls and the area outside. To build a house was to build a world by ordering space. The site of the first house was the place of creation because it was the place of sacrifice. To drive out the victim by killing him decongests the cognitive map and makes cultural differentiation possible. This differentiation is

---

[8] Malbon, *Narrative Space*, 72–75, on the Exodus and the wilderness; "the sea becomes for him as a road, for he walks on it," 165.

first expressed in the primordial difference between the inside and the outside (of the temple), the sacred place and the profane place. The site of the temple is the place of creation, the primordial mountain or papyrus swamp where the god stood to create the world. The myth of creation is the essential etiological myth of the temple, and it extends to all houses. The architectural categories all represent the center—sacred space and sacred time, the sacrifice and the presence—which is creation in the myth, but in the Gospel, chaos.

The most significant general conclusion that Malbon draws from her structuralist investigation is that the normal correlation between sacred space and order on the one hand and profane space and chaos on the other has been reversed. Profanity corresponds to order and sacrality to chaos as, for example, in the case of Jerusalem, where the city proper and the temple mean chaos for Jesus while the environs like Bethany mean order.[9] The reversal of these binary opposites that underlie all oppositions in the structuralist calculus signifies and so corroborates the fundamental critique of the Sacred that is the heart of our hermeneutic of sacred violence. Furthermore, Malbon concludes that the image of the way is the mediator of the opposition between the Sacred and the profane, and, in accordance with the reversal of the categories, the way leads in a reverse direction, away from Jerusalem into Galilee. It is a reverse pilgrimage.

We welcome this corroboration by a structuralist analysis, but must go beyond it in order to do justice to the poetics of place in Mark. We accept the importance of the category of time in the Gospel but aver that the category of space takes precedence in its communicative strategy. We recognize, however, that these two categories can really only be separated for the purposes of discussion, and that in narratology, as in relativity, time and space are one.

The dominant category is that of the way, and it leads in a circle—into Galilee, alongside the sea, over the water and back, down along the river to Jerusalem, through Jerusalem, and back into Galilee. The Gospel as a whole is a hermeneutical circle that one can enter at any point, and its deep structures are circles from which Jesus is driven out, or into which he comes himself or is invited.

Two intersecting circles correspond to the two realms of the Sacred and the kingdom respectively. The center of the circle of sacred violence is the temple and its counterparts, the synagogue and the house. Its chief

---

[9] *Ibid.,* 160.

representative in the plot is the crowd (the sacred center as mob), and faith is to step out of the crowd and follow Jesus. The center of the kingdom is the child in the arms of Jesus (9:33-37). In answer to the disciple's outrageous wrangle about who is the greatest, Jesus forms them into a circle, puts a child at its center, and then takes the child in his arms, saying that whoever receives such a little one receives him, and whoever receives him receives God. The heart of the Gospel is to receive the ones who have no one to defend them and who cannot pay you back. This is the precise reversal of the normal scapegoating tendency to pick on those who are too weak to defend themselves and have no vindicator.

By contrast, at the center of the temple there is nothing. The rending of the veil shows that "there is no there there." Empty space is at the heart of civilization, the child is at the heart of the community of Jesus. There is a rough doublet to this concurrence of a child in the arms of Jesus and the squabble about prestige in the next chapter (10:17), where the welcoming of the children precedes the sorrowful departure of the rich man who could not leave his riches for the kingdom, and the request of James and John for special seats in the kingdom. The theme of how difficult it is to enter the kingdom contrasts with the ease by which the children enter. The disciples try to drive them away, to scapegoat them, but Jesus insists on admitting them. In the next episode, the rich man takes himself away. Prestige and power keep one from the kingdom while the ingenuousness of a child takes one in.

Eccentricity

Jesus replaces the temple in the sense of taking its place, but not at the center. He is *eccentric and thus nonviolent.* Malbon discovered by means of a structuralist analysis what is immediately obvious: Mark reverses the normal assignment of order to the sacred place and chaos to the profane. Chaos, in the sense of nothingness, inheres in the sacred; order, in the sense of loving acceptance, is found in the presence of Jesus. That the center does *not* hold is good news because, when it does, the passionate intensity of the best is more dangerous than the lack of conviction of the worst![10] The Gadarenes find the demoniac, whom they could not chain, sitting peacefully, "clothed and in his right mind" in the presence of Jesus. They had tried to bind him to themselves by the chains of mimetic dependency; he

---

[10] To paraphrase Yeats, *The Second Coming.*

willingly attaches himself to Jesus in love. The crowds find food in the wilderness in the presence of Jesus, and the storm is stilled by the one who walks on the water. All this is radically eccentric!

Time is the favorite category of existentialism, and space, of scientism. The temporal ecstasies of *dasein* and the geometrical figurations of structure constitute the respective opposites of the two epistemologies. The hermeneutic of sacred violence, however, like the image of the way in the plot of Mark, mediates the two categories. The shift from the sacral center is a shift from presence to future, from presentation to re-presentation, and from sight to faith. The weak child at the center of power, over against the emptiness at the heart of the temple, proclaims that, here and now, power presents itself *per contra* and takes place on the periphery. The center has shifted to the margin and presence has mutated into preparation. This is a form of deference.

The interiority of time and the exteriority of space are also mediated by the mimetic construction of the subject. One enters one's own deepest desire through the desire of the mediator. The self is mediated to the self through the other, therefore the way into time leads through space as the way into the self leads through the other. The circularity of the way is the literary counterpart not only of the hermeneutical circle but also of the mutual entailment of two selves in the triangle of desire. Thus, the hermeneutic of sacred violence in all its eccentricity mediates the conflict between time and space and reconciles Via and Malbon without a sacrifice. Time and space are one, on the gospel's way to the future.

6

The Gospel and the Sacred

Girard says that in history we are in travail between the gospel and myth, between the truth of the cross and the mythological lie of the double transference. The biblical texts are also in history and in the same travail. The truth of the gospel is the faith that confesses the reality of power behind the weakness of the servant, and the lie of myth is the reason that explains the necessity of victimage for order. The community of the gospel follows the scapegoat out of the sacred circle along the way of Exodus; the order of sacred violence dwells at the sacrificial center on the foundation of the surrogate victim. The poetics of violence seem to have structured the Gospel of Mark and the poetics of love to have filled those structures with the new gospel energy, but to what extent and in what sense is this the case? The question of the relationship between the gospel and the Sacred must now be posed in terms of the relationship between structure and dynamics at the level of generation. To what extent does the nonsacrificial energy of the gospel change the deep structures of the Sacred at the generative level of the Gospel?

Breaking the Sacred Circle

The clearest sign of new energy infusing and modifying, but not destroying existing structures, is the image of the circle that controls our interpretation. The circle is primarily a sign of the Sacred; it signifies the closedness of the system of violence and the mimetic reciprocity of vengeance. Herod can identify Jesus only as John returned because no one new can enter the circle, and the Pharisees can interpret the exorcistic power of Jesus only as Beelzebub casting out himself. This is the secular attitude of the closed system, and any divinity confined within this system is by definition an idol. The Gospel portrays the new way of Jesus as a circle, but is it the same old circle?

We have already argued that in the world of Mark's reader the circle is actually an upward spiral. Those who walk it with Mark experience a new energy and a new vision. Gradually, they see and perceive, hear and understand. This, however, occurs neither automatically nor perfectly. Misunderstanding and cowardice persist, and so the circle has to be traversed again and again, the Gospel must be read many times and pondered. It is like any classic work that by definition is worth reading often because there is always something more to teach and learn, but it is also more than that. The Gospel achieves a critical advance beyond sacred violence by certain elements in the plot that prevent it from becoming just another violent circle.

These elements are the stupidity, treachery, and blustering cowardice of the disciples, and, climactically, the cry of dereliction from the cross. The disciples symbolize the Gospel's understanding of its community. The parable of the sower, which is key to the interpretation of all parables, tells us that only a quarter of those in the community can be relied on to bear fruit. The disciples do not understand who Jesus is (4:41) because their hearts are hardened (6:52; 8:17). They misunderstand the way of the cross and are as uncomprehending as the crowd (8:32-34). At one pole is Judas, the betrayer outright; at the other is Peter, the betrayer despite himself. The message of the resurrection singles out Peter as a sign that he is forgiven and declares that the faith of the new community can only be based on repentance and forgiveness. Thus, the circle of the Sacred becomes a spiral of grace. The second and subsequent times round we are able to acknowledge our fear and faithlessness because we see that Peter is not rejected, and thus we spiral upward and out of the rut of the Sacred.

The cry of dereliction (15:34) is the decisive caution against Jesusolatry. Had Jesus been a hero of the Sacred, he would have come down from the cross and confounded his tormentors. Then faith would not have been necessary and Christians would have been soldiers in the new model army of the messianic general. Too much Christian theology has simply been propaganda for this general and strategy for his war, interpreting the resurrection as if it were the three-days-delayed transformation of Jesus into a sacred hero. The church has often heroized Jesus, but at its heart the dying derelict has sounded a perpetual protest against such pagan superstition. He followed the way of the servant beyond the pale of faith and hope and God, for the sake of love.

The cross is the final *per contra* disclosure of the power of the non-sacred, nonviolent, nonpresent God. The juxtaposition of the death of Jesus, the rending of the veil, and the confession of the centurion (15:37-39) identifies the decisive event. At the semantic level, the three events have the same meaning; the death is the unveiling of sacred violence and the revelation of God to the Gentiles. To unmask the Sacred is to enable the Gentiles to have faith. For this reason, Jesus "came out" (1:38b) from the synagogue in order to preach the gospel; the coming out and the preaching of the gospel are the same thing. The Gospel of Mark, therefore, undermines the order of the Sacred by entering its center and then leaving for the margins. By confessing that it stumbles around the periphery rather than sits secure at the center, and that its hero is a religious derelict rather than a sacred hero, it makes it impossible for the violence of the Sacred any longer to weave the web of myth over the humanity of its characters. From within the structures of the Sacred, the gospel drains those structures of significance.

This draining is reflected in the Gospel indications of tension between Jesus and the existing order. In 1:40-45, Jesus seethes with anger against the sacrificial system as he cleanses the leper. In the conflict stories of 2:1—3:35, he repeatedly defies religious law and custom until the Pharisees conclude that he must be Beelzebub (3:20-30). He forgives sins (2:5-12), eats with ritual outcasts (2:13-17), rejects fasting (2:18-22), lords it over the Sabbath (2:23—3:6), and repudiates the ties of natural family (3:31-35). Add to this the touching of the bleeding woman (5:24-34) and an array of other facts—missionaries also break the ties of normal family life (6:6-13); inner purity entitles one to withdraw from the sacred system (7:1-23); Jesus goes freely in Gentile lands, and performs healing miracles there (7:24-30); and, climactically, the disciples describe themselves as those who have willingly become outsiders with reference to the Mosaic law as well as to economic security and family relations (10:28-31)—and we have a very strong case for the repudiation not only of the spirit but also of the structures of sacred violence.

These indications of radical restructuring are, however, balanced by the indications of cowardice and misunderstanding, which suggests an ambiguous relationship between stasis and change. This ambiguity can only be mediated eschatologically. It is the result of the tension between the founding mechanism on the one hand and the disclosure of the victim, under the conditions of the present age, on the other. The mechanism is already on the decline because its working is being disclosed to more and more people; nevertheless, it remains in operation, even among those who are conscious of its nature and demands, because there is not yet anything better, and there will not be anything better before the eschaton because the kingdom comes from God and not from us. The community of the kingdom in the present is at best an imperfect anticipation of the future ideal, and the most we can hope for is to manage the communal situation and to purify ourselves as individuals as far as our situation allows. Our eschatological entrapment is well described in Luther's *simul iustus et peccator*.

Yet, in the Gospel, there is a preference for change over stasis. We see the eschatological plight of the community most clearly in the portentous conclusion to the Gospel, "They were afraid" (16:8). Because of fear, they failed to tell the message of the resurrection. Fear inhibits our challenging the structures, and for that reason is the opposite of faith (5:36). To live as the community of the victim within the order of the executioner demands courage to reveal the kingdom *per contra*. Only those who have faith enough to reverse the double transference by changing allegiance from the executioner to the victim can receive the contrary communication of the kingdom and thus gain insight as they read the Gospel again and again and try to live it, while others lose even the little insight that they have (4:11-12, 24-25). "Be careful what you hear, for the measure you give will be the measure you get, and more shall be given you. For whoever has, to him shall be given, and whoever has not, from him shall be taken away that which he has" (4:24-25).

The treatment of the events of the fall of Jerusalem in chapter 13 illustrates the eschatological mediation of the ambiguity between stasis and change. The historical events of the city's fall are not the eschatological events themselves but part of the historical prelude to the eschaton. The eschaton itself lies in the imminent future. The structures of sacred violence are being revealed as the abomination takes place in the holy of holies, but they are not yet destroyed. The process of their destruction may have begun precisely with this radical unveiling, and we may look forward to the continuation of that process; nevertheless, the final denouement will be sudden and miraculous, not the culmination of an amelioration of violence.

Revealing and Reveiling

The phenomenon of "revealing and reveiling"[1] by which insiders become outsiders and vice versa—the disciples misunderstand while the

---

[1] W. Kelber, "Narrative and Disclosure."

centurion understands—also points to the eschatological ambiguity. The realization that we cannot change the structures of sacred violence causes revelation to change to reveiling. The meaning of the death of Jesus is instinctively reveiled because it is too demanding. It shows that the mechanism cannot be stopped in the present but only unveiled, and that we must continue to live as victims among executioners and take the necessary measures to defend ourselves. Out of this realization comes the system of the uneasy conscience that is characteristic of the Christian's political posture, the theory of the just war, and the Christian support for the state and its claim to a legitimate security.

Sacred violence provides the state with its legitimacy and fuels the optimism and idolatry of the patriot. It sanctions the judiciary, justifies class distinctions, bestows prestige on the "best people," and dignifies the executioner. Through the instrumentalities of its high offices, it crucifies the Son of God and forces us who are privy to this secret to support his murderers with our taxes and pretend allegiance to their hypocrisies. Under this pressure, recognition easily turns to reveiling as we fail to accept the truth of the crucified because we cannot endure the tension of a love–hate relationship with the present age.

A Revolution in Values

Gerd Theissen proposes to interpret the tension between the community of the Gospel and the dominant order in terms of a "revolution in values" (*eine Wertrevolution*).[2] Using class as the principle of division, he argues that in the world of the Gospels the lower classes arrogate to themselves the values of the upper classes. These values are principally power, possessions, and culture (*Bildung*),[3] which the Gospel poor claim to have in greater measure than the rich of this age. There is much to be said for this interpretation, especially since it frees us from the assumption that the Gospels show an unreflective preference for the poor and an implacable hostility to the rich. One can speak only of a qualified hostility when the attackers share the values of the attacked and claim to be better representatives of those values. It also enables us to understand why the "heroes" of so many of the parables are rich men or men who display the aristocratic

---

[2] G. Theissen, "Jesusbewegung als charismatische Wertrevolution."

[3] *Bildung* has the connotations of culture in the sense of developed sensibility, refinement, and insight. See H.-G. Gadamer, *Truth and Method*, 10–18.

virtue of generosity.[4] Both sides of the class struggle in the Gospels share the same values, but they understand them differently.

Theissen's analysis supports the static side of the dilemma; it is not the structures that change but the content of the structures. The values of aristocratic virtue and generosity remain admirable; the aristocratic way of achieving them becomes questionable. The analysis must, however, be modified by setting the class confrontation within the more fundamental confrontation between the gospel and the Sacred. The Gospel of Mark is not Marxist, and class is not one of its categories. The primary difference is not between the rich and poor but between the Sacred and the gospel, the circle of violence and the spiral of grace. Once we make the transposition from sociological to religious categories, the ethical demands change. If we know the secret of the Sacred, we are ethically obliged to withdraw support from the structures of violence as far as that is feasible under present circumstances, and that entails not merely a class inversion of values but a substantive change in the values themselves. The change will probably take the form of a deconstruction that acknowledges that there is "no there there," that certain values are only disguised violence. The structures of sacred violence are founded on the lie of the double transference and those who have seen through it know that there is no foundation under them.

Nevertheless, even though they exist by a conspiracy of vanity, like the emperor's new clothes, these structures cannot be dispelled by the voice of the child. That happens only in myths and fairy tales. In the real world of the gospel, vanity still isolates the savior and crushes him beneath the sins of the world. The gospel undermines the Sacred by disclosing it. The responsibility for withholding cooperation from it thus becomes a moral claim on us. In this sense, Via is right to call his exposition of the Gospel of Mark an ethics. What the Gospel reveals of the gospel lays a moral claim on those who see. The proper response to that claim is faith, in the sense of responsibility, trust, and a new way of living. The Gospel of Mark clears that way for us as it parses the poetics of violence and opens up the possibility of faith in response to the gospel.

---

[4] J. Breech, *The Silence of Jesus.*

Appendix
The Generative Mimetic Scapegoating Mechanism

The theory of the generative mimetic scapegoating mechanism (GMSM) is a theory of the nature of desire and its role in social and cultural formation. The modern quest for *an understanding of human desire* can be traced to Georg Hegel's *The Phenomenology of Mind* (1807).[1] Sigmund Freud made the strategies of desire central to psychoanalysis, and Jean-Paul Sartre, to the project of existentialism. The nature of desire was a major concern of French thought after the Second World War and in that context René Girard turned his attention to it. Because he is not a philosopher but a literary critic, he did not pursue his project philosophically but by the interpretation of literary and anthropological texts.

Girard was alerted to the peculiarly triangular nature of desire by the Anselmo and Lothario episode in *Don Quixote,* where Anselmo urges Lothario to seduce his fiancée. To explain this, Girard followed the evidence of literary and ethnographic texts to the Bible, where he claims to have found the problem and its solution plainly set forth. Feodor Dostoievsky and Marcel Proust were particularly influential in the beginning, and now the Bible and Shakespeare have confirmed the insight. Starting from the nature of desire as disclosed in great literature, Girard developed a theory of the Sacred that explains the place of religious institutions in the generation of culture and provides a method

---

[1] See J. P. Butler, *Subjects of Desire.*

129

for the interpretation of texts and cultural formations like ritual, prohibition, and myth.

The method is based on a generative anthropology.[2] Like classical structuralism, it accepts that all the texts of culture are generated by an agency that does not appear as such in the texts. In classical structuralism, this agency is transcendental language, the power of the mind to communicate symbolically. In Girard's method, the generative agency is a psychosocial mechanism that I call the *generative mimetic scapegoating mechanism (GMSM)*. A description of the GMSM tells how desire works to form society. The GMSM is generative because it produces the differences that delineate culture; it is mimetic because it is driven by desire, which functions mimetically; it is scapegoating because it prevents the runaway of mimetic rivalry by means of the surrogate victim; and it is a mechanism because it operates mechanically rather than deliberately.

Because it is generative and not thematic, the traces of the GMSM on the thematic level are not necessarily coterminous with any existing cognitive categories. It is only a theory of sacrifice, or initiation, or the other problematic categories of classical anthropology, in the sense that they are all generated by it, not in the sense that any specific profile of theirs corresponds to its profile. So, for instance, there might be scapegoating texts in which the scapegoat as such does not appear.

The GMSM generates all of culture by managing two fundamental psychosocial propensities, imitation and substitution, in such a way as to reproduce the differentiation that reciprocal violence tends to erase. Imitation leads to reciprocal violence, which has to be directed to create rather than erase differences if there is to be culture and society. The GMSM does this by means of scapegoating, thus generating culture and society by using "good" violence to control the bad.

Imitation is a quality of desire and *vengeance* is the most vivid instance of mimetic desire producing violence. Vengeance is a problem in traditional and modern societies and there have been many rituals and prohibitions to deal with it. The Christian command enshrined in the Lord's Prayer, to forgive if one expects to be forgiven by God, goes to the heart of the problem of reciprocal violence. If vengeance is not controlled or, preferably, abandoned in favor of forgiveness, the distinctions on which individuals and society depend are destroyed by violence.

Scapegoating controls mimetic violence or vengeance. In this discourse, scapegoating does not refer primarily to the ritual of the scapegoat

---

[2] Cf. E. Gans, *The End of Culture.*

described by anthropologists or the Bible (Lev 16). Those rituals are traces of the GMSM, not the GMSM itself. Scapegoating in the GMSM is the psychosocial propensity to relieve frustration by lashing out at someone defenseless, or to avoid responsibility by blaming someone; it is the group's propensity to rescue or cement its solidarity by making an enemy, or the mob's propensity, especially at a time of social unrest, to fall upon a victim. Scapegoating arises from psychosocial propensities that we all recognize in ourselves and in our societies, from the family to the nation. They are phenomena so banal that we seldom reflect on their danger to social order and on the important social mechanisms that control them. In our enlightened democracies, we tend to deny their power over us while they drive our economy and dominate our entertainment industry. Great literature, however, makes us aware of them and Girard's theory explains how they are controlled and directed.

Resentment is the subjective experience of vengeance and scapegoating. It strikes when they fail and the subject is left with unappeased grievances. Then the subject turns the energies of desire upon itself, avenging the self on the self and scapegoating itself. Resentment is the essence of the culture of victimage because it makes the self a victim. Resentment is a powerful ingredient in much modern nationalism, especially the German and Russian kinds.[3]

The theory of the GMSM begins with these shameful and, alas, banal features of human life, and uses them to explain the structure and dynamics of society. It is a social theory of vengeance, scapegoating, and resentment. It makes violence and resentment central to its analysis rather than irrational exceptions. For this reason alone, it is preferable to most other theories of human behavior, which are ethically naive because they do not take sufficient account of these banalities.

I shall present a bare-bones account of the theory without critical evaluation.[4] I cannot present the literary and ethnological evidence, which is in any case entirely convincing. This book is an attempt at a pragmatic justification of the theory, to use it and see how it succeeds or fails in interpreting the text. In this sense, the GMSM is a working hypothesis to be tested by its heuristic power.

---

[3] See L. Greenfeld, *Nationalism.*

[4] The best composite statement of the theory is R. Girard, *Things Hidden,* 3–138. B. Mack gives a brief account in "Introduction: Religion and Ritual," in R. Hamerton-Kelly, *Violent Origins,* 1–70. See also Girard's chapter, "Generative Scapegoating," in *Violent Origins,* and the discussion of it (73–145); Webb, *Philosophers of Consciousness,* 183–225; R. G. Hamerton-Kelly, *Sacred Violence,* 13–62.

The hypothesis, therefore, has two dominant and closely related parts: (1) mimetic desire (reciprocal violence) and (2) the surrogate victim (scapegoating).[5]

Girard develops the hypothesis in a series of books published during the past twenty years, and it is necessary to follow this development from book to book if one is to grasp the theory. To each of the major moments in the theory there corresponds a major book. *Deceit, Desire, and the Novel* (1961; English Trans., 1965) expounds mimetic desire, the starting point of the theory; *Violence and the Sacred* (1972; English Trans., 1977) probes the role of the surrogate victim in the formation of culture; *Things Hidden since the Foundation of the World* (1978; English Trans., 1987) applies both parts to the interpretation of anthropology, psychology, and the Bible; *The Scapegoat* (1982; English Trans., 1986) summarizes and defends the category of the surrogate victim and applies the theory to further texts of persecution and texts from the Gospels; and *Job, the Victim of His People* (1985; English Trans., 1987) uses the theory to give a new interpretation of the book of Job. Girard's latest book, *A Theater of Envy: William Shakespeare* (1991), demonstrates the critical power of the theory to interpret poetry and drama. *Deceit, Desire, and the Novel* treats mimetic desire; in *Things Hidden,* however, Girard speaks less of desire and more of acquisitive and conflictual mimesis. I shall focus on these two works, with some attention to *Violence and the Sacred.*

1. Mimetic Desire (Acquisitive Mimesis)[6]

1.1. How Desire is Mimetic

Desire is mimetic in the sense that it imitates desire, that is, it *copies the other's desire for an object* and not the outward form of the other's actions. Mimetic desire or mimesis is the starting point of the theory. The Platonic tradition in philosophy is based on the separation of mimesis and desire. Mimesis is simple imitation and desire is simple wanting. Girard reconnects mimesis and desire and thus restores the insight of Heraclitus that violence is the source of all. Mimetic desire is violent because it leads to the rivalry of desires. Plato separated imitation and desire because he wanted order and for that he had to eliminate violence. Heraclitus knew

---

[5] J.-P. Dupuy, *Ordres et Desordres,* 125, identifies the two: mimesis is the inclusive category of which surrogate victimage is one form among others.

[6] The best introduction to this part of the discussion is found in Books 1 and 3 of Girard, *Things Hidden.*

that violence could not be eliminated by this kind of metaphysical fiat, that imitation and desire belong together, and that violence is their off-spring. Reconnecting imitation and desire is the fundamental move and it discloses the centrality of violence in the system of desire, which is the human system as such. Everything in the theory follows from this insight.

The model of desire is the "mediator." All the great novelists understand this fact "intuitively and concretely, through their art."[7] Don Quixote, for instance, "has surrendered to Amadis the individual's fundamental prerogative: he no longer chooses the objects of his own desire—Amadis must choose for him. This model, Amadis, is the mediator of desire."[8] Madame Bovary desires through the heroines of the second-rate fiction she reads, and one of Stendhal's *vaniteux* "will desire any object as long as it is already desired by another person whom he admires."[9] Proust's snob is the prisoner of those he wishes to be like, and their disdain of him lashes his admiration of them to greater intensity. Such characters show the mimetic nature of desire, which can only value objects that others already value.

Not only individuals but also society can be the model of desire. One also learns what is desirable from the aggregate of others that is society.

The configuration of desire is therefore triangular. It runs from the subject through the mediator to the object.

1.2. External Mediation

The angles at the base of the triangle of desire can be large or small; the larger they are, the farther the distance between the plane of the subject and the plane of the mediator, and vice versa. When the distance is relatively far, the relationship between the subject and the mediator is one of pure imitation untrammeled by rivalry; Girard calls this the state of external mediation.

1.3. Internal Mediation

When the distance between the plane of the subject and the plane of the mediator is relatively small, the relationship is one of mimetic rivalry; Girard calls this internal mediation.

---

[7] Girard, *Deceit,* 3.
[8] Ibid., 1.
[9] Ibid., 6.

1.4.   Mimetic Rivalry

As the plane of the mediator approaches the plane of the subject–object, rivalry grows with an intensity inversely proportionate to the diminishing distance.

1.5.   The Model/Obstacle (Scandal, Envy, and Hatred)

As the plane of the model approaches the plane of the subject–object, the model gradually turns into an obstacle. The subject is thus sadomasochistically related to the model/obstacle, wanting both to overcome and to be overcome by it. He or she wants to overcome the obstacle and to be overcome by the model, because the model certifies the value of the object while the obstacle contests possession of it.

The *scandal*—a technical term for Girard—is that one and the same person or group plays both roles, of model and obstacle, at the same time. Mimetic desire, therefore, loves the thing it hates and hates the thing it loves, and needs the stumbling block because the obstruction creates the value.

Desire cannot remain in a state of scandal indefinitely. If it cannot escape from scandal by a creative managing of mimesis, scandalized desire eventually loses its equilibrium and falls first into envy and then into hatred. It begins by wishing to be like the rival (external mediation), then wishes to be like and to conquer the rival at the same time (scandal), then simply to conquer the rival (envy), and finally to destroy the rival (hatred). Envy is the stage of the conquered rival; it desires to humiliate and force the rival to witness the triumph.

1.6.   Transcendence

The triangularity of desire means that a human being is structured with reference to transcendence. Human desire is mediated desire: it gets its goal and direction from without, not from within. The state of mimetic rivalry is the pathology of a "deviated transcendence," a desire whose goal or direction should be a truly transcendent spiritual person but instead is aroused by the immanent neighbor. The biblical name for this is idolatry, and its antidote is faith in the unseen God.

1.7.   Metaphysical Desire

In the situation of mimetic rivalry, the object becomes progressively less important. The rivals focus chiefly on each other in a struggle for the being that they mistakenly assume each other has. This is the stage at which the Hegelian analysis of human relationship as the struggle for recognition becomes pertinent. Raymond Schwager refers us to Hegel's idea that desire desires the desire of the other.[10] For Girard, however, desire is imitative and acquisitive; it does not desire the desire of the other as such but imitates the other's desire for an object.[11] As the mimesis progresses toward conflict, desire begins to lose sight of the object and to focus on the other. In the extreme outcome of the mimetic crisis, the object is lost altogether. The desire becomes not merely to possess what the other desires but to possess the being of the other, to *be* the other.

1.8. Substitution

Because the object is now unimportant, several substitutes can serve as the excuse for metaphysical competition, hence the frequent incommensurateness between the trivial cause and the passion of conflict. For the same reason, violence can easily substitute one object for another. The model/obstacle loosens the attachment of both to the object.

1.9. Acquisitive Motivation

Not all acquisitive motivation is mimetic. There is a difference between needs and desires. Needs are the biological requirements of the organism and certain rudimentary psychic requirements like infantile interaction with parents; desires are culturally mediated wants. The major part of human acquisitiveness is, however, mimetic—provoked and defined by the pull of the acquisitive actions and intentions of the other. The phrase "mimetic desire" is, therefore, a tautology: desire is mimetic acquisitiveness, and it can be more or less rivalrous depending on the distance between the planes of the subject and the mediator.[12] This is why Schwager draws the distinction between natural needs and desire in terms of the specificity of the former and the generality of the latter; the desire that is

---

[10] R. Schwager, *Must There Be Scapegoats?*, 35–40.

[11] Ibid., 35–37; Dupuy, *Ordres et Desordres*, 133, distinguishes Girard's position ("un desir *selon l'Autre*") from Hegel's ("un desir *du desir de l'Autre*").

[12] "Desire is what happens to human relationships when there is no longer any kind of resolution through the victim. . . . Desire is the mimetic crisis in itself: it is acute mimetic rivalry with the other which occurs in all the circumstances which we call 'private,' ranging from eroticism to professional or intellectual ambition" (Girard, *Things Hidden*, 288). "We might well decide to use the word desire only in circumstances where the misunderstood mechanism of mimetic rivalry has imbued what was previously just an appetite or need with this ontological or metaphysical dimension" (ibid., 296).

subject to mimesis is "that fundamental desire that forms and defines the total behavior of the human being" which is to be distinguished from hunger or the need for sleep.[13] This fundamental human desire is characteristically cultural.

1.10.   Mimetic Desire's Roots in Phylogeny

Girard first recognized mimetic desire in European novels, Greek tragedies, and certain ethnological sources, and then expanded the insight into a fundamental anthropology and ethology. The question of human nature remains alive and is to be asked and answered in the "domain . . . of the origin and genesis of signifying systems, which in the life sciences is the process of hominization."[14]

Thus, this is a theory of origins that links current human relations with traditional societies and animal behavior. The capacity for imitation is shared by human beings with the higher apes; there is a developmental connection between animal mimicry and human imitation, and the point of hominization might be plotted with reference to the change in this activity. Animal mimicry is also acquisitive and goes through the same process of escalating rivalry as human mimesis. However, animals have instinctual braking mechanisms that prevent the rivalry from becoming group-destroying violence. The weaker animal surrenders and patterns of dominance are established; subordinate animals now imitate dominant ones in noncompetitive areas, without acquisitiveness. Animal mimesis is closely tied to the object and does not develop the metaphysical dimension of a struggle for prestige that human mimesis does.

The human capacity for metaphysical desire might be correlated with the growth of the brain and the extraordinary length of infantile dependency. Humans have more mimetic energy than animals and press the rivalry to the point where the object disappears and the rivalry becomes metaphysical and murderous.

2.   The Surrogate Victim or
Scapegoat (Conflictual Mimesis)

The moment of hominization begins with the disappearance of the contested objects in the midst of mimetic conflict. In Girard's terms,

---

[13] Schwager, *Must There Be Scapegoats?* 235, n. 9.

[14] Girard, *Things Hidden,* 6–7.

acquisitive mimesis becomes conflictual mimesis. The rivals are models/obstacles to each other in a struggle no longer for a specific object but for prestige.

2.1. The Crisis of Differentiation

Rivals come to resemble each other more and more, and as the differences between them are progressively erased they become doubles. What started as a one-way imitation becomes a two-way imitation, each copying the desire of the other until they are identical. The appearance of doubles in a text, the erasure of difference, as, for instance, between the characters of Dionysus and Pentheus in Euripides' *Bacchae,* is a sign that mimetic desire has reached this crisis stage. Distinctions are blurred, animals and humans melt together into monsters, and violence reigns in confusion. This stage of the erasure of differences is the "sacrificial crisis" or "mimetic crisis" and can be seen in the texts wherever distinctions are blurred and one can no longer tell the difference between the sexes or between humans and animals.

The violence generated by mimetic rivalry reaches a climax in the crisis of differentiation and converges on a victim. "If acquisitive mimesis divides by leading two or more individuals to converge on one and the same object with a view to appropriating it, conflictual mimesis will inevitably unify by leading two or more individuals to converge on one and the same adversary that all wish to strike down."[15] We have arrived at the second fundamental human characteristic on which all culture is based, the surrogate victim mechanism.

2.2. The Emergence of the Surrogate Victim or Scapegoat[16]

The mimetic crisis is resolved when the group converges on and kills one victim. The acquisitive mimetic rivalry that drove people apart turns to conflictual mimetic desire, which unites them against the surrogate. The same mimetic violence that divided them as rivals now unites them as accomplices, and what makes the difference is the victim.

---

[15] Ibid., 26.

[16] Girard uses the term "surrogate victim" only for the spontaneous psychological mechanism by which we transfer violence to a victim, and not for ritual transference (ibid., 33). His chapter, "Generative Scapegoating," in *Violent Origins* is the best explanation of the surrogate-victim mechanism.

Instead of all becoming the victim of each, one becomes the victim of all. This happened as a spontaneous event in the system of desire. Its psychosocial traces can be observed in the everyday tendency to make scapegoats bear the brunt of violence. The most significant institutional clue to its existence is the primitive Sacred in its manifestations of prohibition, ritual, and myth. In taking the institutions of religion this seriously, Girard stands in the tradition of Emile Durkheim, especially as it is represented by the English school of social anthropology, pioneered for religion by Jane Harrison and the Cambridge school of Greek historians.[17]

We might imagine the originary scene as follows: In the beginning, the primal horde was wracked by mimetic violence. This violence increased until it reached a crisis point at which the surrogate victim appeared and the mob spontaneously united in killing him. This was the point of hominization. It was the result of the following events: First one pair of rivals, then another rediscovered the object pole of the mimetic triangle as the substitute target for their murderous rage at one another. Some might have discovered it spontaneously; most would have discovered it by imitating the discoverers. Mimesis broke out in a new form: acquisitive mimesis became conflictual mimesis, uniting rather than dividing the community, as all rushed to cooperate mimetically in the killing of the victim. Thus, unanimous victimage played the same role in human community as the surrender of the weaker animal plays in the establishment of dominance patterns among the higher animals.[18]

Gazing at the corpse, the mob's stupefaction turned to awe as it realized that it had just experienced its first moment of unanimity. This reconciliation must have come after a mimetic crisis so severe that the sudden resolution at the expense of a single victim seemed like a miracle. "The experience of a supremely evil and then beneficent being, whose appearance and disappearance are punctuated by collective murder, cannot fail to be literally *gripping*."[19]

---

[17] See F. M. Turner, *The Greek Heritage*, 116–34, cited by A. Henrichs, "Loss of Self, Suffering, Violence," 207–8. Henrichs describes the Cambridge school as "a small circle of historians of Greek religion at the turn of the century who transformed Greek myth and tragedy into a blood-drenched hunting ground for cannibals and ritual murderers and who saw a human substitute for the dying Dionysus in each tragic hero on the Attic stage." J. G. Frazer, of *The Golden Bough* fame, is an important influence behind the school; he was Jane Harrison's teacher.

[18] Girard, *Violent Origins*, 129.

[19] Girard, *Things Hidden*, 28 (emphasis added).

2.3. The Generation of Differences

The erasure of distinctions makes culture impossible, and disordered perception causes monsters to appear, because the differences between humans and animals are no longer clear. This is the *crisis of differentiation* that Girard calls the *sacrificial crisis* or the *mimetic crisis*. Because differentiation is culture's supporting skeleton, there had to be, in the course of development, a way of restoring the distinctions that violence erased, and it had to be a cultural device because prehominid dominance patterns and automatic hierarchies do not work for humans.[20] The cultural device in this case was the *generative mimetic scapegoating mechanism (GMSM)* that arises from within the crisis of differentiation as a spontaneous metamorphosis of the system.[21]

The spontaneous unity created by the surrogate victim is the necessary condition for the reinstitution of differentiation, and differentiation is necessary for culture. Therefore, culture comes from the victim. Mimetic rivalry had erased differences and made the combatants "doubles" of one another. The GMSM, which comes into being as a result of this spontaneous change in the system of desire, first puts an end to the bad violence of mimetic rivalry by the "good" violence of surrogate victimage, and establishes the unity of the lynch mob. Then it uses the difference between the two kinds of violence and the difference between the mob and the victim as the fundamental differences on which to build all subsequent cultural differentiation. Culture comes from the "lamb slain since the foundation of the world" (Rev 13:8), because differentiation ramifies from the victim.

3. The Double Transference

The double transference is the primal misunderstanding by which the mob misidentifies the causes of its disorder and its unanimity. The cause

---

[20] The increased power of imitation in humans can probably be correlated with the growth of the human brain and the consequent enhancement of the imitative energy. In prehominid bands, mimetic rivalry does not reach the point of crisis because the simian brain does not generate the same amplitude of imitative energy as the larger human brain. In animal groups, patterns of dominance can be established within the existing system; human groups need some new ordering factor.

[21] At this point, the link to systems theory becomes evident. See H. Atlan and J.-P. Dupuy, "Mimesis and Social Morphogenesis," and Dupuy, *Ordres et Desordres.* Dupuy's ideas of "tangled hierarchy" (e.g., Escher's "Hands") and "endogenous fixed points" are particularly pertinent here.

of disorder is in fact mimetic rivalry and the cause of peace is the coalescence of that rivalry against the victim. The appearance of the victim
catalyzed the coalescence, but the mob's own mimetic rivalry caused it.
The victim is at most a catalyst and at least only the passive object of the
violence; he or she is not the cause. The mob, however, makes the victim the cause, and by so doing obscures its own violence from itself and
transfers it to the victim. The first illusion is "the illusion of the
supremely active and all-powerful victim";[22] it makes the victim a god,
placing him or her above the group as the transcendent cause both of
order and disorder.

3.1.   The Nature of the Double Transference

The mob transfers its own violence to the victim by the simple misattri-
bution of the cause of unanimity. *This is the critical step, according to the theory, and it occurs spontaneously when violence reaches a certain level of intensity
in the group.* Violence is not repressed and cast off into the unconscious, but
rather it is detached by being transferred to the victim who becomes, as a
result, the god,[23] because of his power to cause and to cure violence. Now
the victim/god is the processor of bad violence into good violence, the
violence of disorder into the violence of order. Thus, the Sacred is the
personification and reification of the mob's violence through the victim.
"Violence is the heart and secret soul of the Sacred."[24]

The transference is double because the mob's violence has two parts:
mimetic rivalry and surrogate victimage. The former causes disorder;
the latter restores order. The victim, in fact, is merely the target and
catalyst of surrogate victimage; as an active cause, however, he also signifies mimetic rivalry. The mob attributes mimetic rivalry and surrogate victimage to the victim, and makes him into the sign of the two
valences that correspond to these two stages of human violence. The
double founding mechanism now operates through the victim; he is
full of mimesis that demands to be appeased by victims. We transfer to
the victim not only our mimetic violence but also our deflecting
mechanism; in theological language, we make him bear both our sins
and the sin of making him bear our sins. It is not we who demand victims; it is he!

---

[22] Girard, *Things Hidden*, 52.

[23] Girard, *Violence and the Sacred*, 136.

[24] Ibid., 31.

3.2. The Victim as Transcendent Signifier

The double transference makes the victim the transcendent signifier. The cadaver is the first object of a noninstinctual attention because of the miraculous peace that attends the victim's death. The cadaver is the sign of peace, and the mob seeks to perpetuate that peace by repeating the sign; hence the imperative of ritual. The cadaver signifies the violence that led to the killing; it is the signifier, and the violence of the mob is the signified. But now the signals are crossed; the cadaver has been made to signify the nonviolence of the group and the violence of the victim.

The victim signifies by the logic of the exception, of the "short straw," or "the odd man out." Structuralist topology demands at least two signs at the beginning because signs only signify with reference to each other; the logic of the victim differentiates by means of the one who stands out from the many, the exception, "the odd man out." The mob and the victim are thus the two poles of the first act of signification.[25]

Because the victim determines human behavior not by means of "what really happened" but through the interpretation that the community transfers to him and that he in turn represents to them, to interpret culture is to decode the double transference. To decode the double transference is to read "all the actual and potential meaning the community confers onto the victim and, through its intermediacy, onto all things."[26] The interpretation of the Sacred is the beginning of the interpretation of culture.

All of culture, then, comes from the surrogate victim by way of this double transference. He is made both the cause and the cure of mimetic disorder (bad violence) and of surrogate-victim order (good violence). His living must have caused disorder if his dying brought order. For this reason, the victim becomes a god, and in that form reflects back these two misunderstandings as the imperatives for prohibition, ritual, and myth.

4. The Products of the Double Transference

The victim processes bad violence into good, disorder into order. Violence passes from the mob, through the victim, and back to the mob. It leaves as violence and returns as hominization, religion, and culture. It leaves as

---

[25] Ibid., 100–1.
[26] Girard, *Things Hidden*, 103.

undifferentiation and returns as differentiation. Thus, the double transference transforms the victim into the Sacred and through the Sacred
generates prohibition, ritual, and myth, which are the fundamental differentiating principles of culture.

4.1.   The Sacred

The center of the Sacred is the victim-become-god-by-the-double-
transference. The double transference gives the Sacred a double valence
of threat and promise corresponding to mimetic rivalry and surrogate
victimage respectively. These are the Girardian counterparts of Rudolf
Otto's *mysterium tremendum et fascinans*. Threat takes the form of prohibition and promise the form of ritual. The two valences represent the
two forms of violence, bad violence that disrupts order (mimetic rivalry) and good violence that establishes it (surrogate victimage). The
Sacred is, therefore, essentially violence.

The Sacred is the transcendental pole of primitive religion. It has been
understood either as an invention of the superstitious mind to provide
prescientific explanations, or as a mysterious real presence apprehended in
the religious attitude. Girard tells us that it is a mendacious representation
of human violence; it is "the sum of human assumptions resulting from
collective transferences focused on a reconciliatory victim at the conclusion of a mimetic crisis."[27]

The element of "the overwhelming" defines the Sacred; it includes
the experience of tempests, fires, and plagues, but its primary content is
violence understood, like these catastrophes, as being outside of normal
human control.

Religious thought conceives of a malevolent quasi-substance polar-
ized around the Sacred.[28] This quasi-substance of the Sacred is the
violence of the primordial murder transformed by the lie of the double
transference into the sanction of cultural order. The polluting power of
the holy, and the prestige of kings, priests, and mythic heroes, is therefore, unacknowledged violence. It pollutes and confuses precisely because it is unacknowledged. All institutions and their hierarchies are
fundamentally sacred structures of organized violence.

The Sacred engenders or destroys cultural structures, but is not itself present in the structures;[29] they are the result of human restraint, a

---

[27] Ibid., 42.
[28] Ibid., 48.
[29] Girard, *Violence and the Sacred*, 241–42.

rational response to an irrational threat. Fear is the motivating power of the Sacred.

Through the Sacred, the double transference generates prohibition, ritual, and myth as the fundamental institutions of cultural order. They are dynamics of the Sacred rather than conscious or unconscious functional strategies of the group. The interdiction of mimicry or the ritual regulation of vengeance, for instance, is not primarily an unconscious judgment of a functional kind but rather a response to and representation of the valences of the Sacred.

4.2. Prohibition

Prohibition corresponds to the mimetic rivalry pole of the double transference and the negative valence of the Sacred. It aims to prevent mimesis. Mimetic conflict is the common denominator of prohibitions, and they all have an antimimetic character.[30] They generally pertain to objects that the community cannot divide peacefully: women, food, weapons, and the best places to live. The prohibition, therefore, derives primarily from the mimetic-rivalry element in the Sacred.

As a dynamic of the Sacred, the common denominator of all prohibitions is fear of mimetic rivalry transfigured by the detour through the Sacred into the fear of the return of the victim to avenge his death,[31] that is, fear of the vengeance of the god. Having been the catalyst of conflictual mimesis that united the group, the victim becomes the sign of prohibition on anything that can disrupt that unity.

The first prohibition and the first differentiation are the same. The transfigured victim is not to be approached, not to be touched, not to be possessed; it occupies a place beyond reach and a line of distinction is drawn between it and every other place. Thus, the first prohibition and the first differentiation are the same; they are the distinction between the victim and the group, the Sacred and the profane. This distinction or fundamental prohibition is the essence both of religion and of law. Prohibition, although principally correlated with the negative pole of the Sacred, is correlated in a secondary way with the positive, ritual pole through the distinction between the Sacred and the profane. The prohibited Sacred place is the place of ritual sacrifice from which the energy of order emanates. Prohibition guards the sacrality of ritual.

---

[30] Ibid., 14, 19.
[31] Ibid., 76.

The two imperatives of prohibition and ritual are curiously contradictory. Prohibition in essence means that one should not repeat any aspect of the crisis; ritual requires that one repeat the whole thing with great care. Prohibition interdicts mimicry, contact with former antagonists, acquisitive gestures toward the objects that caused rivalry, and anything that may reactivate the crisis; ritual deliberately reactivates it, organizes orgies of transgression, and immolates new victims in ways that are thought to repeat the original action.

4.3.   Ritual[32]

Ritual corresponds to the surrogate-victim pole of the double transference and the positive valence of the Sacred. A primary form of ritual is blood sacrifice.[33] Girard sees this as corroboration of the intuition that "there is a relation between the forms of ritual and the universal human tendency to transfer anxiety and conflict on to arbitrary victims."[34] Blood sacrifice is an attempt to repeat the transference of violence onto the surrogate victim under controlled circumstances, and so renew the power of pacification of the original murder. It is generated by the positive valence of the Sacred.

Girard's linking of sacrifice to the surrogate victim does not amount to a theory of sacrifice. The rites that classical anthropologists classify as sacrifice are only one type among many that show traces of the GMSM.[35] Girard stands in the Durkheimian tradition, which sees religion as the primary expression of the power that forms society, and ritual as the essence of religion. For Girard, the Sacred is itself a product of society. The social crisis of violence is prior to the Sacred and to ritual and myth.

A major alternative view, represented in our time by Mircea Eliade, sees religion as a response to the experience of the Sacred as ontologically

---

[32] W. G. Doty, *Mythography,* is a good account of the state of the discussion in myth and ritual studies. For this section see Girard, *Things Hidden,* 48–83.

[33] J. Z. Smith, in Hamerton-Kelly, *Violent Origins,* 202–5, reminds us of the argument that blood sacrifice is not part of the earliest strata of culture but emerges only at the stage of nomadic animal herding. He admits that the evidence is tenuous and difficult to assess. Given that fact, and our general epistemological situation of having to read evidence in the light of our theories (cf. Quine and Ullian, *The Web of Belief*), we see no reason to abandon Girard's claim that blood sacrifice is the first cultural act. There can be no hard evidence for this. It must remain a theoretical postulate.

[34] Girard, *Things Hidden,* 131.

[35] For a convenient treatment of current theories, see Joseph Henninger, "Sacrifice," in M. Eliade, ed., *The Encyclopedia of Religion,* 12:544–57; for Girard's theory of sacrifice, see *Violence and the Sacred,* 1–67.

prior to the human individual or society.[36] Myth rather than ritual is the essence of religion, and both of them are human responses to the manifestation of the Sacred. The word precedes the deed, and myth goes before ritual.

Like the prohibition (cf. 5.2), sacrifice can also be correlated, in a secondary way, with the other (mimetic) pole of the Sacred. Mimetic conflict appears through the Sacred as the "vengeful fury of the divinity,"[37] and this fury has to be appeased. The interpretation of sacrifice as appeasement of the wrath of the god is the essence of the sacrificial lie. The victim actually recalls the god in his role of the surrogate victim, and should, therefore, represent the violence of the offerer. The double transference, however, reverses the order and makes the victim represent the offerer as victim of the god rather than the god as victim of the offerer. The murderer thus appears as the murdered, the persecutor as the persecuted. Sacrifice conceals the fact that the offerer is violent and imputes the violence to the god, pretending that the vengeance deflected onto the substitute is divine and not human. Sacrifice, therefore, reverses the direction of the original action identifying the victim as the executioner and the executioner as the victim.

Sacrifice is therefore the deflection of violence from one target onto another. As part of the double transference, it is the avoidance of responsibility for violence. It is prophylactic. It prevents disorder by removing violence that might otherwise be directed at a member of the group and set the spiral of revenge spinning. It is a device for channeling violence out of the group.

4.3.1. Rules of Ritual Purity

Sacrifice renews the therapeutic effect of the deflecting mechanism by providing a ritual core to which the violence is attracted and from which it flows out again in proper channels.[38] These channels are the rules of ritual purity that keep the various parts and persons of society in their "proper" places. The essential ingredient in all ritual pollution is violence.

Contravention of the rules causes pollution, and the polluting agent is not dirt but violence. "Dirt"—as that which is out of its "proper" place—

---

[36] Eliade, *The Sacred and the Profane*.

[37] Girard, *Things Hidden*, 14.

[38] Doty, *Mythography*, 141: "By ritual retelling of the Creative Acts (*gesta*), the society believes it can make present once again the powerfully creative dynamics of that primal period and so recharge the energies of the present."

is a rationalization of violence. The "proper" place is any place that is so located as not to cause unnecessary rivalry. Thus, the proper place of family members in the subsequent generation is another family. Siblings are too close to each other to avoid mimetic rivalry, and so the laws of incest are part of the sacrificial strategy to inhibit and channel violence.

4.3.2. Liminal Figures

Hyam Maccoby calls attention to the figure of the "Sacred Executioner."[39] The double valence of the sacred victim is also in the executioner; he is the source of both bane and blessing. In him, the status of victim is extended to a living member of the group who by that action becomes a liminal figure. He is the priest, a figure that, along with the king and the mythic hero, is especially associated with the Sacred and therefore regarded with deep ambivalence. These figures represent the "beyond" at the center of society. Their precincts are the forbidden cities, temples, and places of sacrifice where violence is processed into power. Prestige and all the other intangibles of authority that cling to them are the quasi-substance of violence that congeals around the victim. Every king, priest, and hero, therefore, is the victim and the god, an institution for the processing of violence from bad to good.[40]

As the incarnate Sacred, the king is feared and adored, and his perch is always precarious; the oscillation from god to victim takes place suddenly, as many a politician can attest. The shift from adoration to execration usually happens in a mimetic crisis when the community needs to engage the founding mechanism again. Only the double valence of the Sacred can explain the gyrations of political attitude and the extraordinary power of the leader for good and for ill.

The rituals of kingship show the working of the founding mechanism. In the beginning, the king was probably the victim whose period of preparation stretched until he had so much prestige that the community could no longer kill him. He was originally "a victim with a suspended sentence."[41] Kingship rituals often include the king's transgression of especially strong taboos in a moment of ritual chaos that is reduced to order by his enthronement, thus enacting the transformation of violence

---

[39] Maccoby, *The Sacred Executioner.*
[40] Girard, *Violence and the Sacred,* 104–8.
[41] Girard, *Things Hidden,* 52–53.

through the death of the victim, and presenting enthronement as the ritual equivalent of sacrifice.

The king is the living god, and the god is the dead king; the king represents the presence of Sacred power in this world, and the god represents its presence in the "beyond"; the king is correlated with the moment before the death, in which the chosen victim shares the prestige of violence while still alive, and the god is correlated with the moment after the death in which the violence is located in the "beyond." The polysemousness of the GMSM presents now one resource, then another, for the cultural process.[42]

4.3.3. Vengeance

Vengeance is mimetic violence. The principals imitate each other's violent acts. It is a ritual of reciprocity[43] and poses an insoluble problem for the normal economic interpretation of reciprocity, because it is a reciprocity not of gain but of loss. It is the classic instance of the absurd notion that two wrongs make a right, and so cannot be based on a rational calculation of advantage. Vengeance is the reciprocal violence of mimetic desire and could have been dealt with in the section on mimetic desire, but I deal with it here because Girard connects it closely with its solution in sacrifice.

Sacrifice is a mode of appeasement. Violence must be appeased: "If left unappeased, violence will accumulate until it overflows its confines and floods the surrounding area."[44] The acting out of violence that this appeasement demands calls forth reciprocal violence (vengeance), and, unless a way can be found to express violence without vengeance, there can be no appeasement. Sacrifice as a ritual of the surrogate victim is a way to express violence without vengeance by deflecting it from its target onto a victim who cannot retaliate and has no one to avenge him. Sacrifice, therefore, is a ritual cure for vengeance, which in its many overt and covert forms plagues all societies. Sacrifice, and other scapegoating ruses, control vengeance by providing ritual channels for conducting violence out of the group. It functions apotropaically on behalf of the whole community. When it fails, the society falls into a crisis of

---

[42] Ibid., 57.

[43] The sociology developed by Henri Hubert and Marcel Mauss in conjunction with Emile Durkheim is called the sociology of reciprocity. See Mack, in *Violent Origins*, 1–2.

[44] Girard, *Violence and the Sacred*, 10.

vengeance, of violence-provoking counterviolence, culminating in the disorder of the sacrificial crisis.

The sacrificial deflection ruse can be seen clearly in the way some primitives deal with an actual case of vengeance. Girard has observed that among the Chukci the fear of reciprocal violence is so great that they do not allow vengeance to be taken on the one who commits the outrage, but rather on someone else belonging to his cognizant group. In this way, they seek to avoid a symmetry that could become an endless reciprocity.[45]

Such a move is unsatisfactory to a mind used to the rational concept of guilt and punishment, because it results in two random victims and two killers infected by violence, and it violates the canon of individual responsibility. Nevertheless, it makes perfect sense because it protects the groups in question from falling into a spiral of reciprocal violence. It breaks the mimetic symmetry so that the clash is never between violence and violence, that is, between the avenger and the murderer, but always between violence and a victim. Because the victim comes from outside the interchange, he can draw off the violent energy and carry it away from the groups. In this way, the current of violence is broken and the power fizzles dangerously but fruitlessly into the social space made for it by the surrogate victim. The two infected persons are kept from contacting one another and so the possibility of an epidemic of violence is reduced.

A more advanced form of the sacrificial solution is the judicial system. Theoretically, law as the regulator of reciprocity is rationally (rather than ritually) controlled vengeance. The judicial system is a development of the sacrificial control of violence. The violence operating in the judicial system is the "good violence" of the sacrificial order itself. The law represents this order of "good violence," in the form of a controlled reciprocity, which is, in fact, the energy of mimetic desire running in the channels once carved for it by sacrifice.

The initial form of those channels was ritual, as one can see from the stages of the development of law, both logical and actual. Law is the third logical stage of vengeance, in the following sequence: (1) uncontrolled vengeance, (2) ritually controlled vengeance, and (3) law (rationally controlled vengeance). Raymond Verdier, the editor of the most thorough recent examination of the phenomenon of vengeance,[46] calls level two

---

[45] Ibid., 17–28.

[46] R. Verdier, ed., *La Vengeance:* volumes 1 and 2, *La vengeance dans les sociétés extra occidentales;* volume 3, eds. Verdier and J.-P. Poly, *Vengeance, pouvoirs et ideologies dans quelques civilisations de l'Antiquité;* volume 4, ed. G. Courtois, *La vengeance dans la pensée occidentale.* This reference is to Verdier's introductory essay in volume 1, 13–42.

"the vindicatory system" (*le système vindicatoire*), by which he indicates that most primitive societies had prelegal, ritual devices for confining vengeance. He sees this as a refutation of Girard's claim that primitive society was subject to the danger of limitless revenge before the sacrificial mechanism was discovered; but his view in fact confirms Girard, because the sacrificial system is precisely such a ritual vindicatory system.[47]

Gerard Courtois confirms Girard's reading when he notes that the vindicatory system is animated by a strictly retributive idea of justice centered on the victim, not on the perpetrator; the evil to be remedied is that of the situation of the victim.[48] Girard explains this as a result of the idea that the victim is ritually impure, which in turn means that he is the repository of bad violence. He has been contaminated by a violence that has overflowed its ritual channels, and the action that has to be taken at this point seeks to return that violence to its proper channels. This remedial action is usually sacrificial.

Thus, vengeance is an instance of mimetic violence and its control by deflection is a manifestation of the working of the GMSM. The deflection of avenging violence onto someone other than the perpetrator is the surrogate-victim mechanism at work on the level of human relations. It is the logical precursor of law and shows how law and the sacrificial system are genetically related through the Sacred. Law is the myth of vengeance. Violent reciprocity is first ritualized, then rationalized, then mythically transformed into law, and so its violent origin becomes hidden.

4.4. Myths

Mythology is the narrative counterpart of prohibition and ritual, generated by the same mendacious energies of the Sacred. "Myths are the retrospective transfiguration of sacrificial crises, the reinterpretation of these crises in the light of the cultural order that has arisen from them."[49] "Mythological elaboration is an unconscious process based on the surrogate victim and nourished by the presence of violence."[50] Myth, like ritual, represents the founding murder from the point of view of the murderers; only the murderers can make a murder appear as a good thing.

Both Claude Lévi-Strauss and Girard see mythology as a representation of the birth and development of differential thought. They also share the conviction that the passage from undifferentiation to differentiation

[47] M. R. Anspach, "Penser la vengeance," 103–11.
[48] Courtois, in Verdier, *La Vengeance,* volume 4, 32.
[49] Girard, *Violence and the Sacred,* 64.
[50] Ibid., 136.

through a "driving out" is a constant structure in myths. Lévi-Strauss interprets the "driving out" as the expression of the logic of elimination and exclusion by which the mind disencumbers a congested field of perception to make space for differential thought. Mythic thought represents this differentiating process metaphorically, but, because it is incapable of sufficient abstraction, it confuses the process of thought with the process of history and reifies the players.

Lévi-Strauss's topological interpretation leaves some critical points unaccounted for. First, one might ask why the generation of something as antiseptic as his immaculately conceived differential thought should so frequently be represented by a violent expulsion. Second, if the expulsion is for the purpose of disencumbering a field, the expelled must come from within that field; in the myths, the victim comes both from within and from without. Third, his topology cannot account for the conjunction of the chief elements in the structure. Fourth, it cannot account for the fact that the eliminated fragment at first bears a negative connotation and then gains a positive connotation.

Only the GMSM accounts for all the important phenomena. Girard does not simply display the same inability for abstract thought as Lévi-Strauss attributes to the myths and confuse the representations with their referents. He does not infer the communal murder from its representation. Rather, he offers it as a better explanation of the phenomena that both he and Lévi-Strauss observe. Minimally, these are: the negative connotation of the eliminated fragment, the positive connotation of the elimination as such, and the collective nature of the expulsion. It is precisely the conjunction of these three that the topology cannot explain while the hypothesis of an actual communal murder can.

A full Girardian account of the structure of myth has the following features: the theme of undifferentiation; accusations; collective violence; the founding or refounding of culture; the accusation against the mythic hero taken as an incontestable fact.[51] Girard also speaks of the "stereotypes" of persecution: loss of differences, crimes that eliminate differences, the marks of the victim on the alleged authors of the crimes, and the violence itself.[52]

The accusations are transformed into facts because the tellers of the story are the accusers themselves. Mythology's "real project is that of re-calling the crises and the founding murder, the sequences in the realm of

---

[51] Girard, *Things Hidden,* 119.
[52] Girard, *The Scapegoat,* 24.

events that have constituted or reconstituted the cultural order,"[53] and it is always a project of the killers rather than the victim.

Demythification consists in retelling the story from the point of view of the victim, exposing the lie, and revealing the founding mechanism.

Myths have been demythified in the process of history; the great Greek tragedians took the process part of the way, and the Bible brought it to a decisive climax. The Bible is the "essential if not exclusive cause of the dynamic" that sustains Girard's program. Historically, it is the fountainhead of the unprecedented and unparalleled progress of Western civilization away from ritual and myth. The desacralization of culture is the gift of the Bible; we now know the founding mechanism and so can decipher the myths.

4.5. Texts of Persecution

On a spectrum from thorough misrepresentation to complete disclosure, myth stands close to the former pole. With the decay of the sacrificial order, texts come into being that are nearer the midpoint of the spectrum. Girard calls these "texts of persecution." They are especially helpful for identifying the victimage mechanism since in them it is partially revealed. Texts about the persecution of Jews or witches, for instance, betray their mendacity clearly; they accuse their victims of incredible crimes, and, although the texts accept those accusations, we know them to be false. We also know the victims and their sufferings to be real. Thus, we have an instance of the GMSM working before our eyes.[54] The mimetic crisis of violence generates the need for victims, who are accused of incredible crimes and executed, and as a result order returns to the community.

5. The Term "Scapegoat"

The term "scapegoat" is the counterpart in the realm of ritual to the text of persecution in the realm of mythology. In modern usage, it designates both a ritual and a more or less unconscious and spontaneous sociopsychological act. In ethnology, it is a technical term for a ritual; in common usage, it is a term for a psychological act. It is halfway between the pole of concealment and the pole of complete disclosure. The correlation between

---

[53] Girard, *Things Hidden,* 120.

[54] Girard, *The Scapegoat,* 1–44.

psychology and ritual has been inscribed in the language; the Girardian theory has been hidden in plain view for centuries. The psychological precedes the ritual meaning of the term in that the surrogate-victim mechanism is the cause, not the result, of ritual. The scapegoat is not a mere metaphor for an inconsequential psychological phenomenon, but a ritualization of a spontaneous impulse. The "savage mind's" strange idea that guilt can be transferred from one person to another like a physical burden is not the result of an inability to reason, but, on the contrary, a cunning act of rationalization by means of ritual.

Bibliography

Anspach, M. R. "Penser la vengeance." *Esprit* 128 (July, 1987): 103–11.

Atlan, H., and J.-P. Dupuy. "Mimesis and Social Morphogenesis," in *Applied Systems and Cybernetics (Proceedings of the International Congress on Applied Systems Research and Cybernetics)*, volume 3. Edited by G. E. Lasker. New York, 1981.

Bauer, W. *A Greek–English Lexicon*. Chicago: University of Chicago, 1979.

Bleicher, J. *Contemporary Hermeneutics: Hermeneutics as Method, Philosophy, and Critique*. London: Routledge & Kegan Paul, 1980.

Bloch, M. *Prey into Hunter: The Politics of Religious Experience*. Cambridge: Cambridge University Press, 1992.

Borg, M. *Conflict, Holiness, and Politics in the Teachings of Jesus*. Studies in the Bible and Early Christianity 5. New York and Toronto: E. Mellen, 1984.

———. "A New Context for Romans 13." *NTS* 19 (1973): 205–18.

Breech, J. *The Silence of Jesus*. Philadelphia: Fortress Press, 1985.

Burkert, W. *Homo Necans: The Anthropology of Ancient Greek Sacrificial Ritual and Myth*. Berkeley: University of California, 1983.

Butler, J. P. *Subjects of Desire: Hegelian Reflections in Twentieth-Century France*. New York: Columbia University, 1987.

Charlesworth, J., ed. *The Messiah: Developments in Earliest Judaism and Christianity*. Minneapolis: Fortress Press, 1992.

Chilton, B. *The Temple of Jesus: His Sacrificial Program within a Cultural History of Sacrifice*. University Park: Pennsylvania State University, 1992.

Chronis, H. L. "The Torn Veil: Cultus and Christology in Mark 15:37-39." *JBL* 101 (1982): 97–114.

Cochetti, S. "Inquiries into Communication and Action in Nuclear Strategy: A Semiotic Approach 1: The Deterrent System between Communicative and Transcommunicative Action." Unpublished.

Crossan, J. D. *In Parables.* New York: Harper & Row, 1973.

———. "A Form of Absence: The Markan Creation of Gospel." *Semeia* 12 (1978): 41–55.

———. *The Historical Jesus: The Life of a Mediterranean Jewish Peasant.* San Francisco: Harper San Francisco, 1991.

Culler, J. *On Deconstruction: Theory and Criticism after Structuralism.* Ithaca: Cornell University, 1982.

Davies, W. D. *The Gospel and the Land: Early Christianity and Jewish Territorial Doctrine.* Berkeley: University of California, 1974.

Desmonde, W. *Magic, Myth and Money.* Glencoe: Free Press, 1962.

Detienne, M., and J.-P. Vernant. *The Cuisine of Sacrifice among the Greeks.* Chicago: University of Chicago, 1986.

Dodd, C. H. *According to the Scriptures.* London: Nisbet, 1952.

Doty, W. G. *Mythography: The Study of Myths and Rituals.* Tuscaloosa: University of Alabama, 1986.

Douglas, M. *Purity and Danger: An Analysis of Concepts of Pollution and Taboo.* New York: Praeger, 1966.

Dumouchel, P., ed. *Violence and Truth: On the Work of René Girard.* Stanford: Stanford University, 1988.

Dumouchel, P., and J.-P. Dupuy. *L'Enfer des Choses: René Girard et la Logique de L'Economie.* Paris: Grasset, 1979.

Dupuy, J.-P. *Ordres et Desordres: Enquête sur un nouveau Paradigme.* Paris: Grasset, 1982.

Eagleton, T. *Literary Theory: An Introduction.* Minneapolis: University of Minnesota, 1983.

Eliade, M. *The Sacred and the Profane: The Nature of Religion.* New York: Harper Torchbooks, Cloister, 1961.

Eliade, M., ed. *The Encyclopedia of Religion,* volume 12. New York: Macmillan, 1987.

Elliott, J. H. "Social Scientific Criticism of the New Testament: More on Methods and Models." *Semeia* 35 (1986): 1–33.

Funk, R. *The Poetics of Biblical Narrative.* Sonoma: Polebridge, 1988.

Gadamer, H.-G. *Truth and Method.* New York: Crossroad, 1988.

Gans, E. *The End of Culture: Toward a Generative Anthropology.* Berkeley: University of California, 1985.

Girard, R. *Deceit, Desire, and the Novel: Self and Other in Literary Structure.* Baltimore: The Johns Hopkins University Press, orig. work 1961, Eng. Trans. 1965.

———. *To Double Business Bound: Essays on Literature, Mimesis, and Anthropology.* Baltimore: The Johns Hopkins University Press, 1978.

———. *Job the Victim of His People.* Stanford: Stanford University Press, orig. work 1985, Eng. Trans. 1987.

———. *The Scapegoat.* Baltimore: The Johns Hopkins University Press, orig. work 1982, Eng. Trans. 1986.

———. *A Theater of Envy: William Shakespeare.* New York: Oxford University, 1991.

————. *Things Hidden since the Foundation of the World.* with J.-M. Oughourlian and G. Lefort. Stanford: Stanford University Press, orig. work 1978, Eng. Trans. 1987.

————. *Violence and the Sacred.* Baltimore: The Johns Hopkins University Press, orig. work 1972, Eng. Trans. 1977.

————. *Violent Origins: Walter Burkert, René Girard, and Jonathan Z. Smith on Ritual Killing and Social Formation.* Edited by R. G. Hamerton-Kelly, with Introduction by B. Mack and Commentary by R. Rosaldo. Stanford: Stanford University Press, 1987.

Greenfeld, L. *Nationalism: Five Ways to Modernity.* Cambridge: Harvard University, 1992.

Habermas, J. *The Theory of Communicative Action 1: Reason and the Rationalization of Society.* Boston: Beacon, 1984.

Hamerton-Kelly, R. G. *God the Father: Theology and Patriarchy in the Teaching of Jesus.* Philadelphia: Fortress Press, 1979.

————. "A Girardian Interpretation of Paul: Rivalry, Mimesis and Victimage in the Corinthian Correspondence." *Semeia* 33 (1985): 65–81.

————. "Sacred Violence and the Curse of the Law (Galatians 3:13): The Death of Christ as a Sacrificial Travesty." *NTS* 36 (1990).

————. *Sacred Violence: Paul's Hermeneutic of the Cross.* Minneapolis: Fortress Press, 1992.

Hennecke, E. *New Testament Apocrypha* 1. Edited by W. Schneemelcher. Philadelphia: Westminster, 1963.

Henrichs, A. "Loss of Self, Suffering, Violence: The Modern View of Dionysus from Nietzsche to Girard." *Harvard Studies in Classical Philology* 88 (1984): 75–90.

Hooker, M. D. *The Son of Man in Mark: A Study of the Background of the Term "Son of Man" and Its Use in St. Mark's Gospel.* Montreal: McGill University, 1967.

Horsley, R. A. *Jesus and the Spiral of Violence, Popular Jewish Resistance in Roman Palestine.* Minneapolis: Fortress Press, 1993.

Hubert, H., and M. Mauss. *Sacrifice: Its Nature and Function.* Chicago: University of Chicago, 1964.

Jeremias, J. *Jerusalem in the Time of Jesus: An Investigation into Economic and Social Conditions during the New Testament Period.* Philadelphia: Fortress Press, 1969.

Jewett, R. "The Agitators and the Galatian Congregation. *NTS* 17 (1971): 198–212.

Juel, D. *Messiah and Temple: The Trial of Jesus in the Gospel of Mark.* SBLDS 31. Missoula: Scholars Press, 1977.

Kant, I. *Critique of Pure Reason.* Translated by Kemp Smith. New York: St. Martin's Press, 1965.

Kaptein, R., and P. Tijmes. *De Ander als Model en Obstakel: Een Inleiding in het Werk van Rene Girard.* Kampen: Kok, 1986.

Kelber, W. *The Kingdom in Mark.* Philadelphia: Fortress Press, 1974.

————. "Narrative and Disclosure: Mechanisms of Concealing, Revealing, and Reveiling." *Semeia* 43 (1988): 1–20.

Kingsbury, J. D. "The Religious Authorities in the Gospel of Mark." *NTS* 36 (1990): 42–65.

Laum, B. *Heiliges Geld*. Tübingen: Mohr, 1924.

Lévi-Strauss, C. *The Raw and the Cooked: Introduction to a Science of Mythology*, volume 1. Chicago: University of Chicago Press, 1969.

Lincoln, A. T. "The Promise and the Failure—Mark 16:7, 8." *JBL* 108 (1989): 283–300.

Lohmeyer, E. *Galiläa und Jerusalem*. Göttingen: Vandenhoeck & Ruprecht, 1936.

————. *Lord of the Temple*. Richmond: John Knox, 1962.

Lührmann, D. *Das Markusevangelium*. HNT 3. Tübingen: J. C. B. Mohr (Paul Siebeck), 1987.

————. "Markus 14.55-64, Christologie und Zerstörung des Tempels im Markusevangelium." *NTS* 27 (1981): 457–74.

Lühmann, N. *Soziale Systeme*. Frankfurt: Suhrkamp, 1984.

Maccoby, H. *The Sacred Executioner: Human Sacrifice and the Legacy of Guilt*. London: Heinemann, 1982.

Mack, B. "The Innocent Transgressor: Jesus in Early Christian Myth and History." *Semeia* 33 (1985): 135–65.

————. *A Myth of Innocence: Mark and Christian Origins*. Philadelphia: Fortress Press, 1988.

Malbon, E. S. *Narrative Space and Mythic Meaning in Mark*. New York: Harper & Row, 1986.

————. "The Jewish Leaders in the Gospel of Mark: A Literary Study of Markan Characterization." *JBL* 108 (1989): 259–81.

Marcus, J. "Entering the Kingly Power of God." *JBL* 107 (1988): 663–75.

————. "The Jewish War and the Sitz im Leben of Mark." *JBL* 111 (1992): 441–62.

Marxsen, W. *Mark the Evangelist: Studies in the Redaction History of the Gospel*. Nashville: Abingdon, 1969.

Miller, R. J. "The Rejection of the Prophets in Q." *JBL* 107 (1988): 225–40.

Neirynck, F. *Duality in Mark: Contributions to the Study of the Markan Redaction*. BETL 31. Leuven: Leuven University, 1972.

Nickelsburg, G. W. E. "The Genre and Function of the Markan Passion Narrative." *HTR* 73 (1980): 153–84.

O'Keefe, D. *Stolen Lightning: The Social Theory of Magic*. New York: Continuum, 1982.

Oughourlian, J.-M. *The Puppet of Desire: The Psychology of Hysteria, Possession, and Hypnosis*. Stanford: Stanford University, 1991.

Petersen, N. R. "The Composition of Mark 4:1—8:26." *HTR* 73 (1980): 185–217.

Pritchard, J. B. *Ancient Near Eastern Texts Relating to the Old Testament*. Princeton: Princeton University, 1955.

Quine, W. V., and J. S. Ullian. *The Web of Belief*. New York: Random House, 1970.

Ricoeur, P. *Freud and Philosophy: An Essay in Interpretation*. New Haven: Yale University, 1970.

Rumelhart, D. "Notes on a Schema for Stories," in *Representation and Understanding: Studies in Cognitive Science*. New York: Academic Press, 1975: 211–36.

Sanders, E. P. *Jesus and Judaism*. Philadelphia: Fortress Press, 1985.

———. *Judaism: Practice and Belief, 63B.C.E.-66C.E.* Philadelphia: Trinity Press International, 1992.

Schank, R., and R. Abelson. *Scripts, Plans, Goals and Understanding: An Enquiry into Human Knowledge Structures*. Hillsdale: Erlbaum, 1977.

Schüssler-Fiorenza, E. S. "The Ethics of Biblical Interpretation: Decentering Biblical Scholarship." *JBL* (1988): 3–17.

Schwager, R. *Must There Be Scapegoats? Violence and Redemption in the Bible*. New York: Harper and Row, 1987.

Smith, M. *Clement of Alexandria and a Secret Gospel of Mark*. Cambridge: Harvard University Press, 1973.

———. "Clement of Alexandria and Secret Mark: The Score at the End of the First Decade." *HTR* 75 (1982): 449–61.

Smith, S. H. "The Role of Jesus' Opponents in the Markan Drama." *NTS* 35 (1989): 161–82.

Steiner, G. *Real Presences: Is There Anything in What We Say?* Boston: Faber and Faber, 1989.

Stemberger, G. "Galilee—Land of Salvation," in W. D. Davies, *The Gospel and the Land: Early Christianity and Jewish Territorial Doctrine*, 409–38.

Sternberg, M. *The Poetics of Biblical Narrative*. Bloomington: Indiana University Press, 1985.

Stetkevych, S. P. "Ritual and Sacrificial Elements in the Poetry of Blood-Vengeance: Two Poems by Durayd ibn Al-Simmah and Muhalhil ibn Rabi'ah." *JNES* 45 (1986): 31–43.

———. "The Ritha' of Ta'abbata Sharran: A Study of Blood-Vengeance in Early Arabic Poetry." *JSS* 31 (1986): 27–45.

Strack, H. L., and P. Billerbeck. *Kommentar zum Neuen Testament aus Talmud und Midrasch*. 6 volumes. Munich: Beck, 1926.

Sylva, D. D. "The Temple Curtain and Jesus' Death in the Gospel of Luke." *JBL* 105 (1986): 239–50.

Taylor, V. *The Gospel according to St. Mark*. London: Macmillan, 1957.

Theissen, G. "Jesusbewegung als charismatische Wertrevolution." *NTS* 35 (1989): 343–60.

Tuckett, C., ed. *The Messianic Secret*. London: SPCK, 1983.

Turner, F. M. *The Greek Heritage in Victorian Britain*. New Haven: Yale University Press, 1981.

Verdier, R., ed. *La Vengeance*. Paris: Cujas. Volumes 1 and 2, *La vengeance dans les sociétés extra occidentales,* 1980 and 1986; volume 3, eds. R. Verdier and J.-P.

Poly: *Vengeance, pouvoirs et ideologies dans quelques civilisations de l'Antiquité,* 1984; volume 4, ed. G. Courtois: *La vengeance dans la pensée occidentale,* 1984.

Via, D. O. *The Ethics of Mark's Gospel—In the Middle of Time.* Philadelphia: Fortress Press, 1985.

Webb, E. *Philosophers of Consciousness.* Seattle: University of Washington, 1988.

Wilder, A. *Jesus' Parables and the War of Myths.* London: SPCK, 1982.

Williams, J. G. *Gospel against Parable: Mark's Language of Mystery.* Bible and Literature 12. Decatur: Almond, 1985.

Wraede, W. Das Messiasgeheimnis in den Evangelien. Goettingen: Vandenhoeck & Ruprecht, 1913.

Yeats, W. B. "The Second Coming." 1920 from *Selected Poems of William Butler Yeats.* Franklin Center: The Franklin Library, 1979: 133–34.

Index of Names

159

Index of Subjects

Index of
Ancient Sources

APOCRYPHA

NEW TESTAMENT